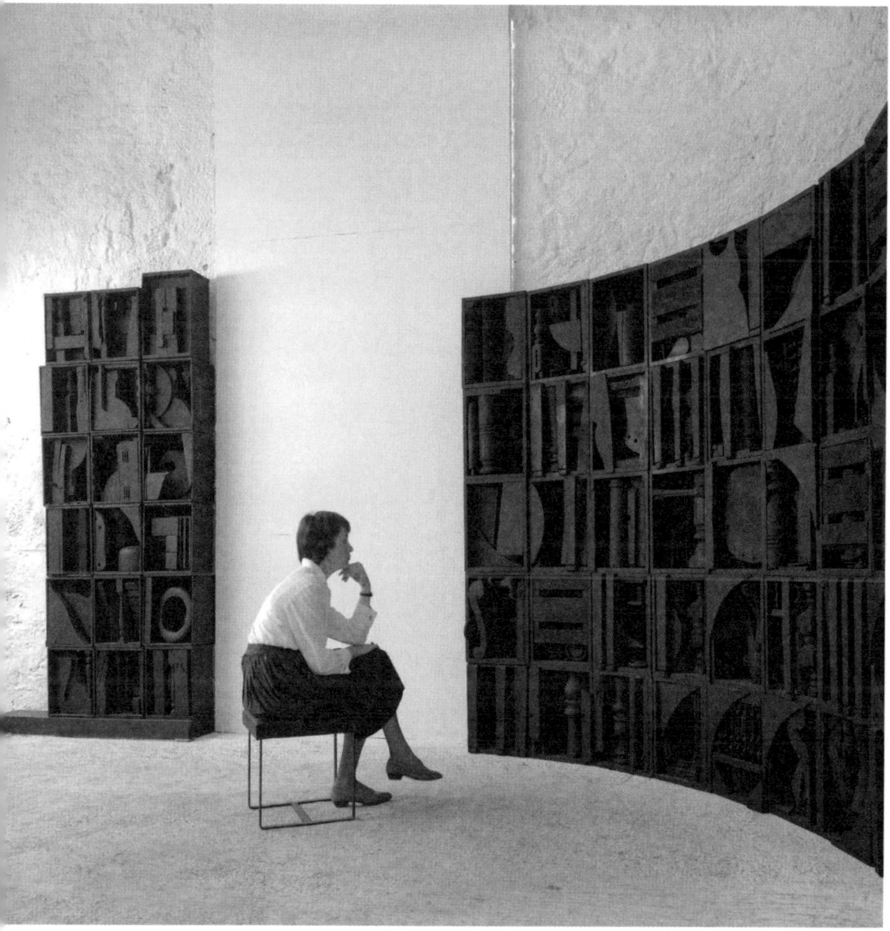

Mission and Commission

documenta
and the Art Market
1955-1968

Mela Dávila Freire

* Daniel Spoerri, letter to Dieter Roth, September 2, 1958, quoted by Katerina Vatsella, *Edition MAT: Die Entstehung einer Kunstform*. Bremen: H. M. Hauschild, 1998, p. 15.

'Art must be cheap,
but still only for the few.'
Daniel Spoerri*

Contents

Preface

[1] Walter Grasskamp, 'For Example, documenta, or, How is Art History Produced?' in *Thinking About Exhibitions*, Reesa Greenberg, Bruce W. Ferguson, and Sandy Nairn, eds., Routledge, London, 1996, pp. 48-56

documenta's early days were bumpy and difficult. The first four exhibitions, held between 1955 and 1968, experienced structural and financial challenges which threatened, not once, but several times, to upend the project entirely. But thanks, in part, to public approval and increasing projection, the challenges were overcome each time and documenta managed to steady the course, holding exhibitions every four years at first, and then, from 1972, every five years. Today, sixty-seven years later, just as documenta 15 is about to open, the Kassel exhibition has become an international event of the first order that is widely anticipated and eagerly scrutinised. Its impact on the art world, especially in the West, is powerful and profound, and coverage is reaching mainstream media – if only fitfully and superficially.

Each new documenta generates rivers of ink in the form of reviews, analyses, comments and critiques – favourable, negative, thoughtful, scathing – that dissect the curatorial concepts at play, the choice of artists and works, the inflexions of the exhibition display, the public programme, the pedagogical approach, and so many other aspects of interest to art history and criticism. Monetary issues also receive ample attention, with questions asked such as how big the budget is, how sound the investment has been, and, of course, if the subject arises (and the fact is that it does, routinely, although the general public is quick to forget), by how much the painful deficit has grown this time and who should be made accountable.

However, to date, there have been relatively few studies that have analysed from a historical and comparative perspective the organisational apparatus sustaining an artistic event of such magnitude: its institutional framework, evolution, economic implications and, notably, the relationship each successive edition has forged with its socio-political situation. This is so despite the fact that from the moment the initial ideas outlining the first exhibition began to take shape, documenta has never turned away from its surrounding circumstances. In 1996, Walter Grasskamp noted: 'In its historiography, documenta is seldom seen in the larger context of its time, but is regarded as a unique event, a stroke of genius of Arnold Bode – which it was in many ways, but not without antecedents. To reconstruct documenta's prehistory in the context of the postwar German and European art scene is work still to be done and might lead to levelling its singularity perhaps a bit.'[1] In 2022, more than twenty-five years later, whether because of the difficulty of putting a long and complex history into perspective, or because the power of its artistic proposals tends to overshadow all other aspects, or simply because of its gigantic scale, the fact is a deeper exploration of the organisational arrangement behind documenta still remains to be done.

Among the many questions that continue to invite analysis, one in particular stands out, namely, documenta's financial implications and how they have played out on various levels. These include the sources of funding, of course, but also the project's links with private sponsorship and its relationship – direct or indirect, deliberate or accidental – with the art trade. It is precisely this last aspect that *Mission and Commission: documenta and the Art Market 1955-1968* sets out to explore.

I first began the research that gave rise to this book while carrying out a commission from the Deutsches Historisches Museum in Berlin, in connection with the preparations for the show *documenta: Politics and Art*, which ran from June 2021 to January 2022. Initial enquiries into the funding of the early documenta exhibitions brought to light an interesting concatenation of instances where the vicissitudes of the organisation interwove with a paradigm shift which, after World War II, would thoroughly change the Western art market. Certainly, many of the key events shaping this sequence were known already, at least to scholars; but what was missing was an attempt to extricate these events from the grand narrative of documenta's history and present them, properly contextualized and interrelated, in a sequence of their own.

This was my goal as I sat down to write this book. Rather than uncover hidden facts, *Mission and Commission* seeks to throw a different light on the progression of documenta through its first four editions by adopting an angle that has not been seen before. Thus, through a revision of documenta's history, from its genesis in the spring of 1955 to the aftermath of the crisis that shook the fourth edition in 1968, a new story has emerged in which for the first time some lesser-known characters and events are brought out of the shadow of documenta's main narrative and given centre stage.

In this story, multiple levels intersect and combine: the budgetary demands of a project whose scale would repeatedly exceed even the most optimistic expectations of its organisers; the shaping of new models of consumption that accompanied the 'miracle' of West Germany's economic recovery; the birth and expansion of an international network of art galleries; and the consolidation of artists' publications, editions and multiples as an artistic genre, partly thanks to galleries' own initiative and partly as a negative reaction to galleries' new role as 'middlemen' between artists and the public.

Many friends, family, colleagues have contributed to this research in the most diverse ways. To all of them I extend my sincere thanks for their help and support: this book exists in large part thanks to them. I also wish to highlight the invaluable help of the archivists and librarians who have accompanied me on this project, always willing to respond in the best way to my requests for assistance.

To recount the story that I felt was worth telling, I decided from the start to put at the heart of it the voices of its protagonists, as they have reached us today via the various documentary sources that I had at hand. Many of these sources can be found in the documenta archiv, whose collaboration has been crucial for this research; but also in the Federal Archive (Koblenz), the archive of Porzellanikon Museum (Selb), the Municipal Archive of Cologne, the Zentralarchiv für Deutsche und Internationale Marktforschung - ZADIK (Cologne), the archive of the Louisiana Museum of Modern Art (Humlebæk), the Deutsches Literaturarchiv in Marbach and, of course, the archive of the Galerie Der Spiegel in Cologne. The delicate task of reconstructing personal profiles and past events through the traces preserved in these archives has been the greatest challenge, and also the greatest source of satisfaction, of writing *Mission and Commission*.

This book is dedicated to my dear children, Flavia and Lino, who have borne my endless hours of writing with patience, complicity and inexhaustible good humour.

How it all began:
the post-war period, Kassel and the 'Bode-Plan'

[1] Helmut Schelsky, *Die skeptische Generation. Eine Soziologie der deutschen Jugend.* Munich: Eugen Diederichs Verlag, 1957

The 1950s was a complex time in West Germany, marked by the economic, social and spiritual reconstruction effort following the disaster of the Second World War, and by vertiginous and profound transformation. The decade began with the country in a state of devastation and exhaustion. The partition into two and subsequent creation of the Federal Republic in May 1949, based on the model of a parliamentary democracy, was followed by a harsh winter in which unemployment figures rose to over two million, concentrated mostly in areas of the country with already high numbers of refugees and displaced persons. When food rationing, introduced at the beginning of the war, in 1939, was finally lifted in early 1950, the country's economy and labour market had all but collapsed.

However, the new Federal Republic would soon enter a period of rapid growth, stimulated by a range of factors. On the international level, the country partook of the economic dynamism generated by industrialised countries' expansion of foreign trade as a consequence of the outbreak of the Korean War (1950-1953). In turn, domestic commerce was revitalised thanks to the swift rebuilding of housing and infrastructure, the modernisation of the workforce and an exponential increase in demand for consumer goods. Additionally, Germany began to receive funds from the Marshall Plan (1948-1952), the economic aid package extended by the United States government to accelerate reconstruction, modernise production and promote trade in war-torn Western European countries, and in so doing prevent the spread of communism and advance capitalist interests. While the Federal Republic was not the greatest beneficiary of the plan – Britain and France received more – and the true impact of the Marshall Plan on the German economy is still a matter of debate, there can be no doubt that this aid played a significant role in its recovery.

Thanks to the combination of these circumstances, by the end of the 1950s the German 'economic miracle' was well under way: the Federal Republic was expanding rapidly and had reached full employment. Certain sectors of production even faced a labour shortage, which led to a massive influx of foreign workers in the following decade.

In the political arena, from 1949 onwards the Christian Democratic Union (CDU), led by Chancellor Konrad Adenauer, strung together one coalition government after another as adulthood came to a generation of post-war *baby boomers* – a social group baptised by sociologist Helmut Schelsky as the 'sceptical generation',[1] less politically motivated and more focused on their own material well-being and prosperity. For the new middle classes, the automobile became *the* must-have mode of transport and a powerful class signifier as well as a formidable sector of industry;

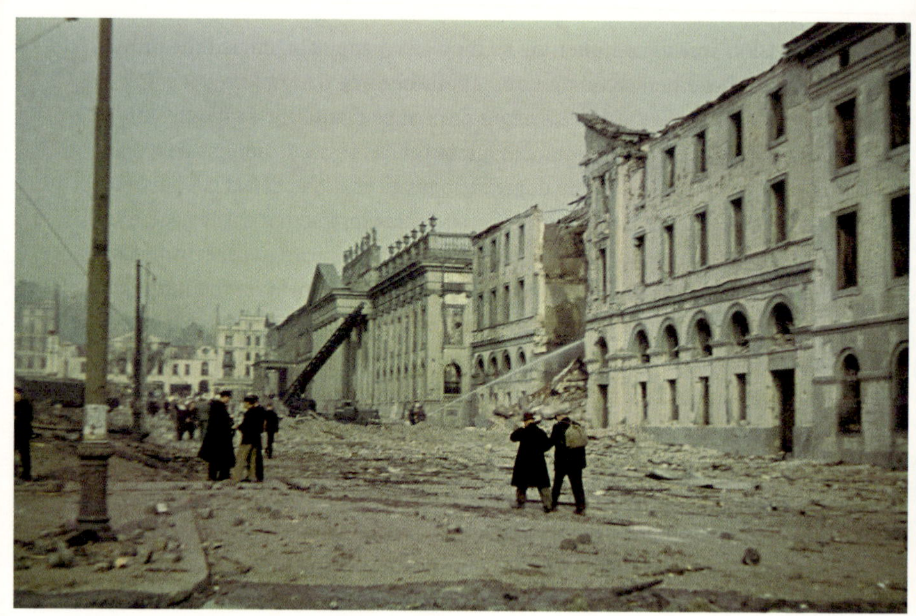

Putting out the flames in the Fridericianum
after an airstrike, October 22, 1943.
Photo: Friedrich Unkel / Kassel Stadtarchiv.

television spread its influence, so much so it soon challenged the printed press for hegemony; and tourism rapidly became the preferred leisure model. In absolute terms, society's level of education rose significantly and unleashed a new passion for consuming cultural goods and products.

The apparent calm in domestic politics after the decades of instability that had led to the horrors of National Socialism and the carnage of World War II nonetheless concealed substantial difficulties. These stemmed from both the geostrategic position the Federal Republic held on the international political chessboard and the country's own determination to rebuild internally, an endeavour that would require addressing the tensions between purification and assimilation but which, as it turned out, was undertaken in rather a half-hearted way, to say the least.

On the geopolitical level, the increasingly strained relations between the United States and the Soviet Union, which had led to the partition of Germany into two halves, placed the Federal Republic in the eye of the storm of the emerging Cold War – an ideological, political and economic conflict of profound and far-reaching consequences which saw each side devote huge economic and human resources to their respective strategies of infiltration, espionage and counterintelligence throughout this and the following decades.

Internally, 'denazification' efforts had had mixed results in the two Germanys. While the Democratic Republic had worked hard to persecute Nazism in the post-war period, in the Federal Republic similar efforts, led by the Allied forces in 1945, had begun to run out of steam as early as 1946 and were officially terminated in 1951 with much weaker results than in the eastern half of the country. As a result, in the following years a considerable number of middle- and high-ranking professionals who had held positions of responsibility under the National Socialist regime were gradually filling the institutions of the new Federal Republic, something that one sector of German society saw as a pragmatic solution while another condemned it as a major capitulation that was both politically and socially reprehensible.

All of these tensions inevitably had a major impact on the reconstruction of cultural and artistic life in the Federal Republic. The re-establishment of cultural normality was proceeding apace, driven by economic growth and rapid social transformation as well as by the importance it was given at the time. Far from being a minor or fringe issue, culture was seen as having the potential to contribute to the great concerns of the time, notably the political re-education of the citizenry and the rehabilitation of the country's battered image both at home and abroad. Clearly, such potential could not be squandered, and to milk the cultural capital, institutions had various mechanisms at their disposal – among them art exhibitions, which would come to occupy a prominent position.

Exhibitions as propaganda was not a new idea. In fact, it rested on a strong tradition dating back to the mid-nineteenth century, when the first such event, conceived explicitly to show 'the advance of progress' from a nationalistic perspective, was mounted on no fewer than eleven separate occasions. The last, entitled *Exhibition of the Products of the Agricultural and Manufacturing Industries*[2] and held in Paris in 1849, was the direct forerunner of the *Great Exhibition of the Works of Industry of all Nations*,[3] which opened two years later in London, inaugurating a long series of Universal Exhibitions that have continued to this day. Although the main attraction of these shows initially lay in the public presentation of scientific and technical advances, with the turn of the century, and especially from 1930 onwards, they began to incorporate more and more cultural content, while new events began to spring up in which art played an important role because of its relationship with industry, as did other creative fields such as design, applied arts and architecture. The Milan Triennale, first held in 1936, is the perfect example in this respect.

Indeed, some of the most important cultural events of the Third Reich were art exhibitions. In Munich, on July 18, 1937 Adolf Hitler opened the first *Great German Art Exhibition*,[4] for which an important number of paintings and sculptures were chosen for their affinity with the National

[2] *Exposition des Produits de l'industrie agricole et manufacturière*, Champs Elysées, Paris, June 1 to July 30, 1849.

[3] *Great Exhibition of the Works of Industry of all Nations*, Crystal Palace, Hyde Park, London, May 1 to October 15, 1851.

[4] *Große Deutsche Kunstausstellung*, Haus der Deutschen Kunst, July 18 to October 31, 1937.

[5] *Entartete Kunst*, Municipal Archaeological Institute, Hofgarten, Munich, July 19 to November 30, 1937. This first presentation was followed by displays in Berlin, Leipzig, Düsseldorf, Salzburg, Hamburg and Vienna, among other cities.

[6] Excerpt from Hitler's opening speech at the *Great German Art Exhibition*, quoted in Kathrin Engelhardt, 'Die Ausstellung Entartete Kunst in Berlin 1938. Rekonstruktion und Analyse'. In Uwe Fleckner (ed.): *Angriff auf die Avantgarde. Kunst und Kunstpolitik im Nationalsozialismus*. Munich: De Gruyter Akademie Forschung, 2007, p. 95.

[7] The *Erste allgemeine deutsche Kunstausstellung* was held from August 25 to October 31, 1946, in the Stadthalle Nordplatz in Dresden. Among the members of the jury selecting the works was the art critic and historian Will Grohmann, who would later become a member of the documenta Board for its second and third editions (1959 and 1964).

[8] Sculptor and member of the selection committee Herbert Vorwahlsen, quoted in Ruth Heftrig, 'Narrowed Modernism. On the Rehabilitation of Degenerate Art in Postwar Germany'. In Olaf Peters (ed.), *Degenerate Art. The Attack on Modern Art in Nazi Germany, 1937*. New York: Prestel and Neue Galerie – Museum for German and Austrian Art, 2014, p. 270.

Socialist idea of 'good art'. Its counterpart opened the following day barely a few hundred metres away: the exhibition *Degenerate Art*[5] displayed a selection of confiscated avant-garde artworks that the National Socialist regime viewed as the embodiment of quite the opposite, that is, the moral and aesthetic degradation to which the artistic avant-garde had descended. These two exhibitions complemented each other in that they showed the public the merits and demerits of the aesthetic tastes of the National Socialist regime in two opposing groups: 'official art' on the one hand and 'pseudo-art' on the other which, in Hitler's own words, was the work of 'cultural pre-historics and chatterers [who], for all we care, can return to their ancestral caves and there apply their primitive international scratchings'.[6] The public success of these two art events was undeniable: while the former attracted over half a million visitors in its first edition, the latter saw an estimated two million plus flock to its Munich presentation alone, and several thousand more on its subsequent tour of German and Austrian cities.

The dark impact of *Degenerate Art* was not limited to its immediate time frame and context. Its sinister echoes would continue to reverberate after the end of the war in a series of 'aftershocks' – exhibitions that set out to counter, more or less explicitly, the postulates on which the National Socialist exhibition had been based. The first took place just after the end of the Second World War, in 1946, in the Soviet Occupation Zone. The *First General Exhibition of German Art*[7] was presented in Dresden with the dual purpose of rehabilitating artistic modernity after its suppression by the Nazis and reconnecting German art with the pre-war avant-garde, and deploying 'propaganda in favour of the unity of Germany'.[8]

In keeping with this second objective, the works exhibited at the *First General Exhibition of German Art*, many of whose authors had featured in *Degenerate Art*, came from almost all the occupied zones of the country. However, history was moving in a different direction, and this inclusive model would quickly be replaced by other selection criteria more reflective of the tensions playing out on the geopolitical chessboard, and the fierce ideological battle that had begun between capitalism and communism quickly spread to the realm of art, finding its equivalent in the clash between abstraction and realism. From 1949, when the division of Germany into two countries became, to all intents and purposes, a reality, the *First General German Art Exhibition* would continue to be organised only in the eastern half of the country. Its sequels were the *German Art Exhibitions*, which went on until 1988, attracting a significant number of visitors. The term 'general', however, was dropped from the title, since only art produced in the German Democratic Republic and officially endorsed by the communist regime was accepted, and this generally pertained to the trend or style known as 'socialist realism'.

In the Federal Republic of Germany, on the other hand, as in the entire Western bloc, abstraction came to be seen after the Second World War as an artistic language characterised by self-determination and political disinterest and therefore distinctive of 'free' states, in contrast to realism and figuration, which were considered to be at the mercy of the propagandistic will of dirigiste and indoctrinating states. This politically polarised perception of artistic movements emanated from several sources, but one that proved particularly instrumental was the American propaganda apparatus, which in the 1950s used the MoMA's International Traveling Exhibition Program to spread its messages about the moral excellence of abstraction. The director of this programme, Porter C. McCray, bolstered by the substantial resources flowing from the Rockefeller Brothers Fund, deployed in Europe an intense campaign of abstract art exhibitions that reflected his own ideas about the political role that American art should play in the moral reconstruction of the West. Indeed, Porter McCray deliberately used the programme to contribute 'a fundamental element to the image of the democratic "free world" with which the United States was dialectically attempting to debunk the USSR's "totalitarian" vision of culture'.[9] Years later, McCray summed up the situation thus: 'Before World War II there were, in essence, two competing visions of the future that dominated the

[9] Paz Guevara, 'Exhibition as Medium for Geopolitical Operations: Digging Up the Exhibitions of the Congress for Cultural Freedom'. In Anselm Franke, Nida Ghouse, Paz Guevara, and Antonia Majaca (eds.), *Parapolitics: Cultural Freedom and the Cold War.* Berlin: Haus der Kulturen der Welt and Sternberg Press, 2021, p. 282.

[10] Porter McCray, 'The (Re) Invention of Postwar Modernism'. Quoted in Anselm Franke, Nida Chouse, Paz Guevara and Antonia Majaca, ibid. pp. 279-281.

[11] Borys Groys, 'The Cold War between the Medium and the Message: Western Modernism vs Socialist Realism', *e-flux Journal*, no. 104, November 2019. See also Alfred H. Barr, Jr., 'Is Modern Art Communistic? On the contrary, says an expert, it is damned in Soviet Russia as it was in Nazi Germany'.

In *New York Times Magazine*, December 14, 1952, p. 22. In this article Barr was reacting to the barrage of criticism that artistic modernism was also receiving from the ranks of Western capitalist society, defending it as the true expression of individual freedom.

[12] Paz Guevara, op. cit., p. 287.

[13] The exhibition, held from October 12, 1951, to February 24, 1952, was spread out across four venues: Museo Nacional de Arte Moderno, Museo Arqueológico, Palacio de Exposiciones del Retiro and Palacio de Cristal. Some of the works subsequently travelled to Barcelona. The Biennial was held on another two occasions: in 1954 in Havana and in 1955 in Barcelona, the latter coinciding with an exhibition of American painting organised by MoMA's Traveling Exhibition Program.

public sphere in Europe: one defined by traditionalism and nationalism and the other by modernism and internationalism. The first option, having been overwhelmingly embraced, inevitably led to the war and to a level of destruction previously unknown to humanity. [...] After the war, when it became clear to Europeans that modernism was the only promising option remaining, MoMA's interpretation of modern art was brought back to Europe.'[10]

The association of modern art movements with specific political currents was not an invention of the Cold War but rather the simplification of a complex constellation of associations that had been forming since the irruption of the avant-gardes at the beginning of the twentieth century. Boris Groys has pointed out that 'Before World War II the fascists saw modern art as an ally of communism, communists saw it as an ally of fascism, and the Western democracies saw it as a symbol of personal freedom and artistic realism – as an ally of both fascism and communism. This constellation defined postwar cultural rhetoric. Western art critique saw Soviet art as a version of fascist art, and Soviet critique saw Western modernism as a continuation of fascist art by other means. For both sides, the other was a fascist.'[11] It was a convoluted political assimilation of artistic currents that – paradoxically – upheld as a bastion of Western culture and its bourgeois values the art of the early avant-garde, which in its day had arisen in opposition to those very same bourgeois values.[12]

Some of the repercussions of this complex web of connotations and accusations against the art of modernity that existed prior the Second World War continued into the post-war period. An example of this is the violent reaction of the more conservative – and more anti-communist – sectors of fascist Spain to the inclusion of Abstract Informalism among the currents officially accepted by the Franco dictatorship, a regime which, of course, also used art exhibitions to spread political propaganda. In 1951, around the same time that MoMA's Traveling Exhibition Program was about to launch its campaign promoting abstract art as *the* art form of the 'free world', the Institute of Hispanic Culture, an arm of the Spanish dictatorship, opened the First Spanish-American Contemporary Art Biennial in Madrid, which Franco attended personally.[13] This show marked a turning point in the dictatorship's cultural policy, which now officially endorsed abstraction through numerous initiatives. But the display of the Informalist current of abstract art for the first time in an official context provoked tremendous indignation in some sectors of society, as an open letter written by the then director of the Prado Museum, Fernando Álvarez de Sotomayor, makes abundantly clear. Addressing a hypothetical 'President of the

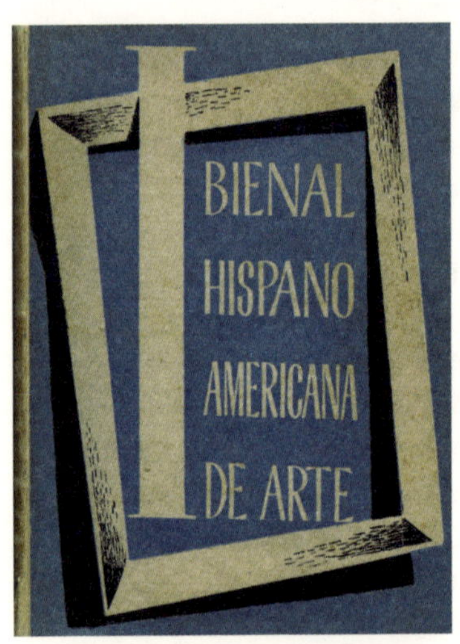

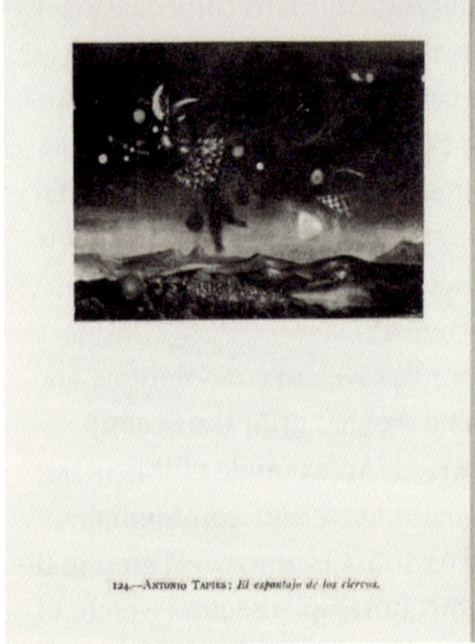

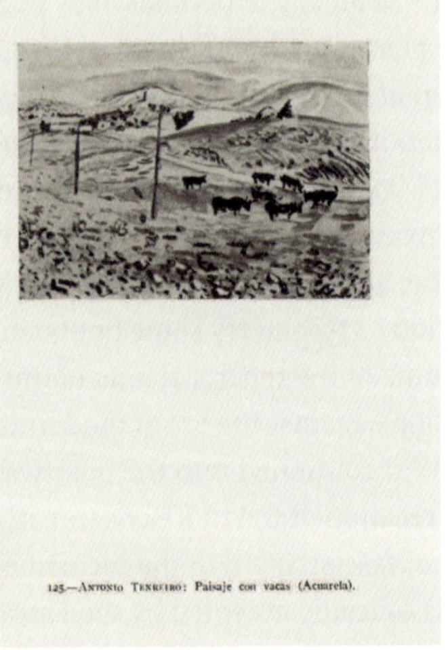

I Bienal Hispanoamericana de Arte. Madrid:
Gráficas Valera, 1951. On the left, Antoni Tàpies,
L'espantall del cérvols. Animal nocturn, 1949.

[14] Miguel Cabañas Bravo, *La Primera Bienal Hispanoamericana de Arte: arte, política y polémica en un certamen internacional de los años cincuenta*. Doctoral dissertation, Universidad Complutense de Madrid, 1991. [http://hdl.handle.net/10261/11455, retrieved in January 2022].

[15] Harald Kimpel, *documenta: Mythos und Wirklichkeit*, p. 168. Cologne: Dumont Buchverlag, 1997, p. 168.

[16] Heinz Lemke, letter to Theodor Heuss, August 16, 1954, documenta archiv, AA, Kassel, d01, 20, fol. 75.

[17] First held in Hanover in 1951.

Psychiatric Section of the College of Doctors', he irately demanded to know if '[the Informalist painters] who paint like this are perpetuators of Socialist militias; enemies of God, order and Christian society, sold to Judaism, Freemasonry, Communism and other such things'.[14]

In the debate about political associations with contemporary art trends which shaped the official cultural policies in the Cold War in the 1950s, other issues were no less complicated. The West's propaganda attacks against the Soviet bloc on social, economic and cultural fronts were further intensified by the conservative and extremely anti-communist bias that the presence of the former National Socialist contingent brought to federal institutions, and, to a lesser extent, by the anti-democratic and imperialist leanings of a sector closely linked to the Christian Democratic Union, which in pseudo-Christian vein, sought to reinstate a monarchical-clerical order in Europe based, at least in part, on ethnic arguments.[15] From the 1950s onwards, notions such as 'Western identity' and 'Western culture' gained currency, borne along by all these impulses and often significantly charged with anti-communist innuendo; and by extension, it included the concept of 'Europe', which the Nazis had already used with clearly racist undertones when referring to the European cultural legacy that needed saving from the Soviet threat.

This was the situation when, in the summer of 1954, the President of the Federal Republic, Theodor Heuss, received a letter inviting him to sponsor an art exhibition, the preparations of which were still very much in the pipeline. 'Dear Mr. President,' the letter began, 'The Member of the Bundestag August-Martin Euler will have already informed you of our plans here in Kassel. We have founded a society which would like to hold a large exhibition of "Twentieth Century Western Art" to coincide with the Federal Garden Show in 1955. Our intention is to show the development of Western art since 1908, or thereabouts, through a selection of three to five masterpieces by Europe's most important artists, and thus reveal our common Western identity.'[16]

This letter, and others like it addressed to senior figures in the federal government and to various officials in the Hessian regional government, had been sent from the location of the upcoming edition of the Federal Garden Show: the city of Kassel. Before the war, Kassel had boasted a major armoured vehicle manufacturing facility, but the prolonged bombing raids spanning from 1940 to March 1945 destroyed 80% of its buildings and infrastructure and left thousands of fatalities and displaced persons in their wake, causing the loss of almost half of its 200,000 inhabitants. It was hoped that the Federal Garden Show[17] would not only showcase the latest

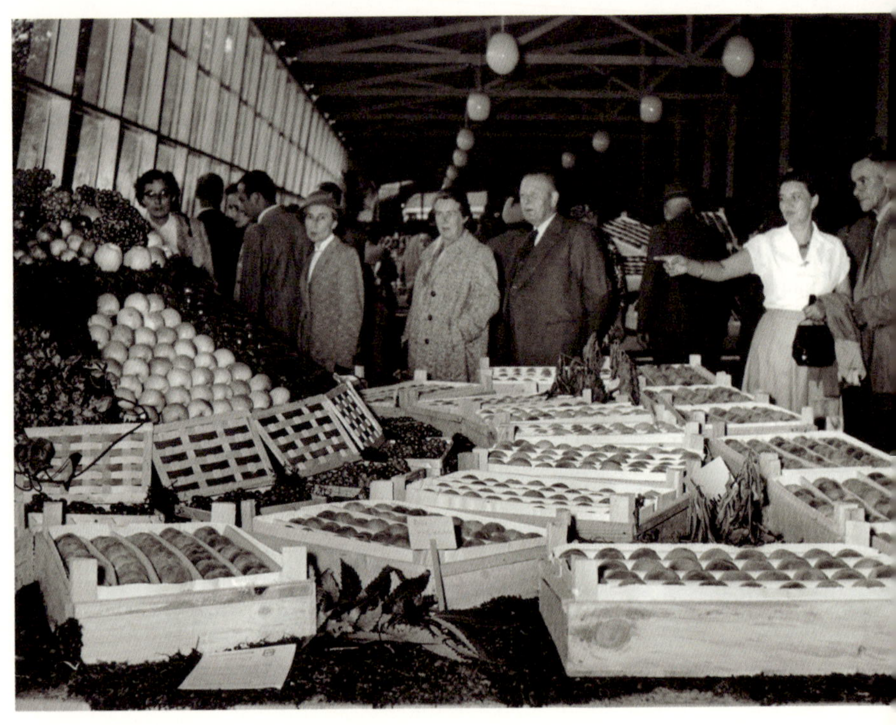

The Orangerie during the Federal Garden Show
in Kassel, August 1955.
Photo: Teubner / Bundesarchiv Koblenz.

[18] To this day, these remain the Garden
Show's two main missions. [https://www.
bundesgartenschau.de/ueber-die-dbg/unsere-
geschichte.html, retrieved January 2022]

[19] Heinz Lemke, letter to the Magistrate of the
City of Kassel, July 23, 1954, documenta
archiv, AA, d01, 20, fol. 65-68.

[20] Harald Kimpel, op. cit., p. 166.

[21] Heinz Lemke, letter to Ludwig Preller, April 7,
1954, documenta archiv, AA, d01, 20, fol. 33/34.

developments in horticulture, but also act as a motor for urban development for each of its venues,[18] and so the decision to hold the 1955 edition in Kassel was undoubtedly a strategic move to accelerate the pace of the city's recovery. Indeed, it was also a necessary move, as reconstruction in Kassel was not progressing as fast as it was in other German cities. To a large extent, this lag was due to the division of the country into two, as a result of which Kassel, once in a relatively central geopolitical position, was now only 30 km from the border with the new Democratic Republic. In other words, it was no longer in the centre but on the periphery of the new Federal Republic.

In fact, the city's new peripheral position was an argument put forward in one of the many letters sent out from Kassel in the summer of 1954 aimed at securing support for the incipient exhibition project about which President Heuss had been informed. Making a virtue out of necessity, the letter, addressed to the municipal magistrate, played up the advantages the enclave offered for directing propaganda at the communist half of Germany: 'As a city that sits close to the border with the East, a cultural city that has been severely destroyed but is now being reborn, and as the site chosen for the great Federal Garden Show in 1955, Kassel seems to us particularly suitable for proclaiming this powerful message of spiritual reference. Perhaps the primacy of the spirit can be revealed more effectively from the presently uncompromising situation of this small city, hard hit but nevertheless rising anew, than from Venice or Paris.'[19]

The sender of these letters was a society that had been constituted only a few months earlier, on April 28, 1953, under the legal form of a non-profit association, the purpose of which, its statutes declared, was 'the preparation and realisation of the exhibition *Western Art of the Twentieth Century,* to be held on the occasion of the 1955 Federal Garden Show in Kassel'.[20] Although originally called the 'Society for *European* Art of the Twentieth Century', the name had soon been changed for the purely practical reason that 'Americans are more willing to lend works by German artists who have become American and no longer represent European art, but American art. The Americans, for their part, are happy to be counted as Westerners'.[21] Given the ideological baggage attached at the time to the concept of a 'common Western identity', it would have been hard not to notice a political intention implicit in the name change.

Who were the members of this society? Its board of trustees represented a broad cross-section of Kassel society: its chairman was the agricultural entrepreneur Heinz Lemke – signee of the letters – and its vice-chairman was Erich Lewinski, former president of the municipal court. Also sitting were politicians such as Bundestag members Adolf Arndt, Ludwig

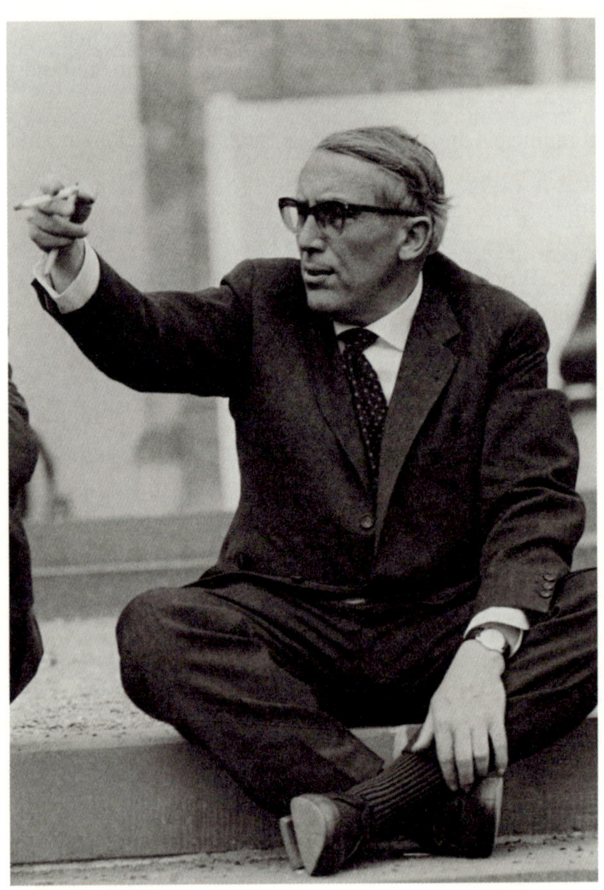

Arnold Bode, ca. 1960.
Photo: Klaus Meier-Ude / documenta archiv.

[22] https://www.documenta-bauhaus.
de/en/institutionen/76/gesellschaft-
abendlandische-kunst-des-xx-jahrhunderts-
e-v [retrieved January 2022].

[23] Mattern had taught at the school since 1947
and had been actively involved in its refounding.
The city's former art school had been forced to
close before the war due to the economic crisis.

Preller and August-Martin Euler, the president of the Hessian regional government, Fritz Hoch, the district administrator, Hans Kuprian, and the Mayor of Kassel, Lauritz Lauritzen; and professionals from the public and cultural spheres at municipal and regional levels, such as the editor-in-chief of the *Hessisch Niedersächsiche Allgemeine Zeitung* Hilde Roemer-Bergfeld (the only woman in the group); the art historian and curator of the Hessian Regional Museum, Herbert von Buttlar; the director of the German Design Council in Darmstadt, Ulrich Gertz; the head of the Kassel State School of Crafts, Stephan Hirzel; the director of the Municipal Theatre, Manfred Schaffner; the director of Kassel's public art collections, Hans-Erasmus Vogel; and the architect Robert Völker.[22]

Although these high-ranking representatives of the local community had joined the Society to back the initiative, the idea of the art exhibition for which they were seeking support had not come from them but from the artistic context of the city. Shortly before, Hermann Mattern, a town planner and landscape designer with experience in previous editions of the Federal Garden Show, had been commissioned to design the 1955 edition in Kassel. Mattern, who at the time was a lecturer in landscape planning in urban environments at the city's State College of Crafts,[23] knew that previous Garden Shows had featured a small section devoted to sculpture, and wished to emulate the experience by including a fine arts exhibition in his design. When he shared these thoughts with his fellow teachers at the school, one of them, Arnold Bode, was so captivated by the proposal he there and then enthusiastically pledged all his support for it.

Arnold Bode was born in Kassel in 1900. The son of a modest furniture manufacturer, he was the eldest of four brothers, two of whom would go on to become architects. After a brief period as a soldier in World War I, he studied painting and design at art school and then devoted himself to painting and organising exhibitions. In 1930, he moved to Berlin to take up a post as a teacher of drawing and decorative design at the Städtische Werklehrer-Seminar, a teacher training college that followed many of the ideas developed in Weimar by the pre-war Bauhaus. That same year, he became a member of the Social Democratic Party.

His Berlin period was to be brief, however. In 1933, with the rise to power of the Nazi Party, Bode fell from grace. He was dismissed from his job and his paintings were removed from the museum collection in Kassel they had been part of until then. He worked on occasional projects and commissions until 1939, when he was drafted into the army. The heavy bombing raids on Kassel in 1943 utterly wrecked his home and a fire ravaged his studio destroying most of his paintings. Bode never painted again. At the end of the war, after a short incarceration in an American detention camp in Bavaria, he returned to Kassel and began taking part in initiatives designed to revive the local art scene, including the refounding of the State School of Crafts, where he took up teaching again, in 1949. He combined this occupation with an increasing number of commissions for industry as an industrial, graphic and product designer. Over time, as clients began to ask him for artistic advice, his already versatile professional profile would evolve in multiple directions, one of which was the programming of an art gallery opened by the Göppinger Plastics company in Frankfurt in 1956.

Thanks to his inexhaustible interest in art, his many business commissions and his outgoing and friendly personality, over his lifetime Arnold Bode built up a broad network of friends and contacts, both personal and professional (and often both at the same time) across a wide range of fields. This proved useful, not only when executing his commissions, of course, but also when giving form to the countless projects and ideas he came up with, for which he deployed his infectious enthusiasm to win the support he needed to carry them out. Archive records prove that Bode's stream of ideas flowed ceaselessly for decades, and although many of them never came to fruition, those that did would leave a significant mark.

Together with other friends and fellow artists, in 1946 Bode had founded the Hessian Secession in Kassel, dedicated to organising exhibitions and artistic activities that probed the boundaries between 'pure' art and the applied arts. The group had a short existence – barely two years – but it was important because it established operational guidelines that Bode would use again later. In 1953, when Mattern asked him to organise a large art exhibition for the Garden Show, Bode immediately rallied friends and acquaintances and mobilised them into what would become informally known as 'Club 53'.

Apart from Herman Mattern, Club 53 included the museum curator Herbert von Buttlar and the sculptor Hans Mettel, who was now teaching sculpture and directing the Städelschule in Frankfurt and whose work had

[24] Heinz Lemke, letter to Theodor Heuss, op. cit.

[25] Julia Voss, 'Kassel 1955: How Documenta Almost Never Happened. The History of Events Leading to the Most Successful German Exhibition and How it Came About'. In Raphael Gross, Lars Bang Larsen, Dorlis Blume, Alexia Pooth, Julia Voss and Dorothee Wierling (eds.), *documenta: Politics and Art*. Berlin: Deutsches Historisches Museum and Prestel Verlag, 2021.

[26] Werner Haftmann, *Malerei im zwanzigsten Jahrhundert*. Munich: Prestel Verlag, 1954.

[27] Carlo Gentile, 'Der Krieg des Dr. Haftmann'. In *Süddeutsche Zeitung*, June 6, 2021.

[28] Arnold Bode, 'Bode-Plan', cover letter with exposé to the Mayor of Kassel, January 19, 1954, documenta archiv, AA, d01, 20, fol. 8-12.

been labelled 'degenerate' by the Nazis. They were joined shortly after
by local personalities and together they formed the Society for Twentieth
Century Western Art, which would act as the legal organising body for
the exhibition. Moreover, Bode and his group also began to contact art
professionals with invitations to participate in the project. 'A working
committee composed of leading representatives of art history and museums,
as well as artists from the Western area, will soon convene and begin
preparatory work,'[24] read the letters of presentation sent out in the summer
of 1954. They would soon be joined, on a more informal level, by Kurt
Martin, director of the Kunsthalle Karlsruhe, and Alfred Hentzen, director
of the Kestner-Gesellschaft in Hannover. Finally, to give the project a more
theoretical profile, in the autumn of 1954 Bode travelled to Italy to meet
Werner Haftmann,[25] a young art historian whose most recent book, *Painting
in the Twentieth Century*,[26] was becoming the great publishing and academic
success of the time.

Werner Haftmann was twelve years younger than Bode and had
studied art history in Göttingen and Berlin. After completing his doctorate in
1936, he had moved to Florence to work as assistant director of the German
Institute of Art History, joining the NSDAP (National Socialist German
Workers' Party) a year later. He remained in Italy during the war, enlisting in
the army there and, as recent revelations have shown, playing a diligent role
in the persecution and extermination of Italian rebels,[27] something he would
be very careful not to ever mention after the war. Following a brief spell in a
detention camp, Haftmann was released in 1946 and he settled in Bremen
before moving to Hamburg where, from 1950, he taught art history at the
School of Fine Arts and wrote art criticism for the weekly *Die Zeit*.

Before the war, Haftmann had shown a penchant for German
Expressionism, but from 1945 he began to develop a new set of theoretical
precepts which he set out in *Painting in the Twentieth Century*, immediately
attracting Bode's attention. In particular, Haftmann's claims that
abstraction was *the* art form of modernity, and that artistic creation should
be independent and radically separate from politics (a notion that resonated
with the political mood of the times), would both deeply influence the
content of the early documentas, whose theoretical and historiographical
framework Haftmann would oversee.

With Haftmann on board, then, the exhibition project's theoretical
basis was cemented and a historiographical perspective added to the general
concepts that Bode had already been defining for some time. The documenta
archiv has at least two typed versions of a text several pages long entitled
Bodeplan, or 'Bode's Plan', in which some of these outlines and initial

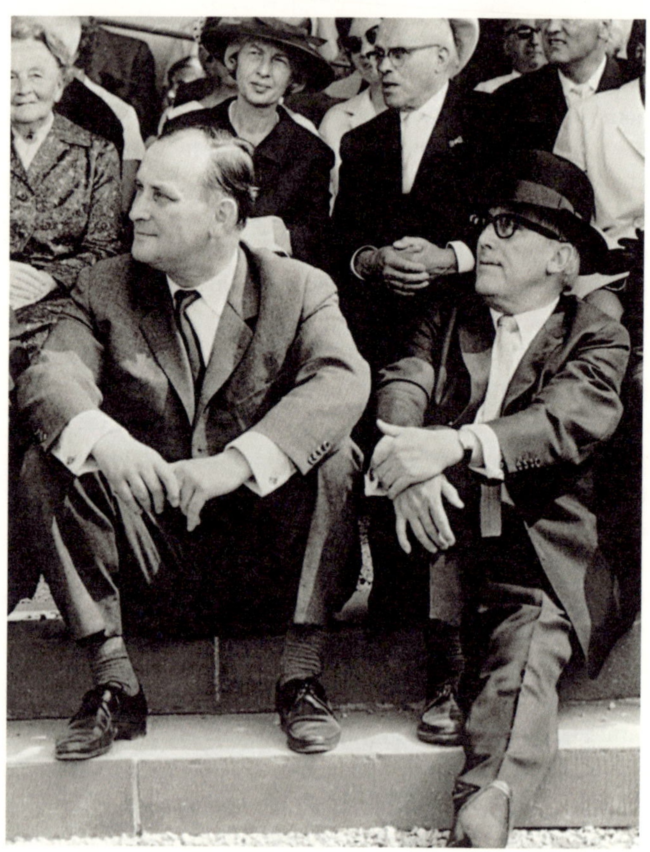

Werner Haftmann and Arnold Bode in
documenta III, 1964.
Photo: Wolfgang Haut / documenta archiv.

[29] Ludwig Mies van der Rohe, 'Museum for a Small City'. In *Architectural Forum* no. 78, 1943.

[30] Early presentations of the project had included an ambitious list of international experts who were to act as advisors to documenta, but the list was dropped as preparations progressed. Among them were Willem Sandberg, director of the Stedelijk Museum in Amsterdam; art historian and curator Jean Cassou; poet and philosopher Herbert Read; and Alfred Barr, director of MoMA. See Heinz Lemke's letter to the Magistrate of the City of Kassel, op. cit.

reflections are set down.[28] Neither version is dated but we can assume they were written in the second half of 1953, as fragments of them appear in a letter Bode sent to the Mayor of Kassel on January 19, 1954.

Bode's plan had ambitious goals, the viability of which could only be guaranteed – as Bode himself pointed out to the Mayor – if regional and federal institutions as well as local authorities also got involved. Bode argued that an art museum has the potential to be a social catalyst and that exhibition events can represent collective values and aspirations. Guided by these ideas, he conceived his exhibition project as a 'total event' that encompassed not only the visual arts, but also poetry, theatre, music, industrial design, interior design and film. From this perspective, it was clear that the success of the project depended not only on the selection of works and the programme of activities, but also on the way the works were displayed. 'The first problem is to establish the museum as a centre for the enjoyment, not the interment, of art', Mies van der Rohe had declared in 1943.[29] The care and attention that Bode put in to designing the exhibition layout and the space around the exhibits would prove to be revolutionary aspects of the show that was just beginning to take form, and whose actual curatorial team was in fact rather smaller than the official documentation suggested,[30] comprising only of art historians Werner Haftmann, Alfred Hentzen and Kurt Martin, artist Hans Mettel, curator Herbert von Buttlar (acting as secretary) and Arnold Bode himself, who, in addition to his design work, breathed boundless energy into the team.

Where the money came from: state and private funding

[1] Hein Stünke, 'Arnold Bode'. In *Jahresring 78-79. Literatur und Kunst der Gegenwart*. Stuttgart: Deutsche Verlags-Anstalt, 1978, p. 269.

[2] Ibid.

[3] Heinz Lemke, letter to Theodor Heuss, op. cit.

[4] Heinz Lemke, letter to Ludwig Preller, op. cit.

Charisma, energy and resourcefulness are some of the virtues often cited in relation to Arnold Bode's legendary personality and his role as the 'founding father' of documenta and, more broadly, in relation to the success of his ambitious initiatives, even those that initially seemed unviable, disproportionate or, at best, impractical. In contrast, little mention is made of Bode's peculiar indifference to the question of how his initiatives should be financed. Indeed, he was not one to allow himself to be easily constrained by such matters, and perhaps such an indifference to money played a part in the success of his achievements. Archival records and colleagues' testimonies confirm that funding issues did not tend to limit the scope of his plans: '[Bode] didn't wait for the money to come through first... He would go ahead with preliminary meetings and discussions to get the project rolling.'[1] Such enthusiasm, however, was not without its drawbacks, as 'the public administration did not always like this'[2] – something that must have surely been problematic. Because, at the time that Bode and his team were beginning to float their proposal, the only structure capable of bearing the estimated costs was, precisely, the public administration, at its various levels: municipal, regional and federal.

In 1954, the art exhibition project that Bode and his group presented to institutional representatives was met with scepticism, which increased the further away from Kassel their offices were. Nor did the vagueness of the plans in those early days do much to further their cause. When the Society for Twentieth Century Western Art began work in August of that year, not only did the exhibition lack a title, but neither its contents nor its financial viability were clear, however much the letters from Kassel stated that the federal government, the Hessen region, the city of Kassel and 'other partners'[3] (without specifying which) were already providing the necessary financial backing. The reality was that at that point only the City of Kassel had explicitly pledged its cooperation, and the substance of the exhibition was still quite nebulous. It would be months before a clear picture began to emerge.

The determination of Bode and his colleagues did not waver, however, and in the second half of 1954 the exchange of correspondence between the Society for Western Art of the Twentieth Century and the highest political and economic authorities of the Federal Republic gathered pace. Depending on the specific interests of each addressee, different reasons were put forward to justify the project. So the City Council and the Hessian regional government were persuaded of the timeliness of holding an ambitious art exhibition in the city because 'an object of lasting importance had to come to Kassel one day'.[4] For the Federal Ministry of Pan-German Affairs, created in

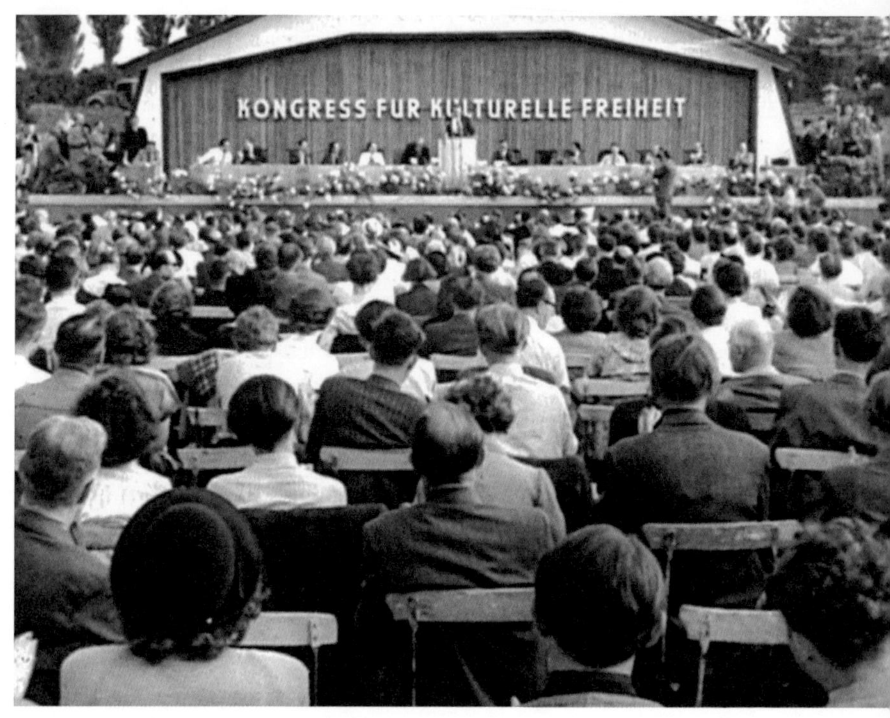

Congress for Cultural Freedom, Berlin, 1950.
Film still from the US Information Agency
documentary *Germany – Rebirth of a Nation*, 1959.
Courtesy of Historiathek, Munich.

5 Arnold Bode, 'Bode-Plan', op. cit., fol. 2.

6 Heinz Lemke, letter to Ludwig Preller, December 11, 1954, documenta archiv, AA, d01, 20, fol. 99.

7 Arno Hennig, letter to the Society for Western Art of the Twentieth Century, December 24, 1954, documenta archiv, AA, d01, 20, fol. 102.

8 Willi Stoph [former Federal Interior Minister], letter to the Mayor of the City of Kassel, January 10, 1955, documenta archiv, AA, d01, 20, fol. 103/104.

1949 to smooth over diplomatic relations between East and West Germany but in reality the vehicle of a sustained, largely undercover, anti-communist propaganda campaign, it was the Federal Republic's proximity to the border with East Germany that was put forward as the main justification. The Federal Foreign Office, in turn, was told that the absence of an institutional structure for art in the Federal Republic (the pre-war one having been completely dismantled) was actually a propitious situation for a peripheral city without a significant contemporary art collection. All these reasons had already been listed in the *Bodeplan* some time before: 'Kassel is *the* German city predestined for such an exhibition. Kassel lies in the border zone, most of it has been destroyed and it is working very hard on its reconstruction. Commemorating the idea of Europe with an art exhibition only thirty kilometres from the border constitutes an exemplary act of symbolic importance. Kassel is not conditioned by the existence of any artists' associations or political-artistic entanglements. Kassel deliberately chooses not to be tied to any established tradition, as this would immediately lead to the formation of factions. With this exhibition, whose fundamental ideas may expand with time, Kassel wants to start a tradition.'[5]

However, despite all their efforts, by December 1954 no significant progress had been made and the schedule was already running very much against the organisers. 'The matter is, of course, very problematic. Professor Bode's trips abroad now depend solely on this initial money, which naturally represents a risk, because in the worst case, we might bring back negative responses from museums and artists' studios. But let's remain hopeful...'[6] Buoyed by brazen optimism, the Society stepped up pressure in December, but the imprecision of their plans continued to hinder them. On Christmas Eve 1954, the Hessian Minister of Education addressed the Society in these terms: 'I wish to repeat that I can only support the release of the proposed substantial subsidy from state funds if I am sure that an exhibition of the highest standards of quality will be held. [...] I therefore urgently recommend that you advance your preparations so that a definitive plan can be submitted within a foreseeable timeframe.'[7]

But help soon came in the form of the symbolic patronage bestowed on the project by Theodor Heuss, President of the Federal Republic and an amateur painter, and things began to move in the right direction. The first positive response to the Society's persistent requests reached Kassel in early 1955, when the federal authorities 'welcomed the project – the Federal Ministry of the Interior, for the bearing it is expected to have in terms of international projection and representation, and the Federal Ministry of Pan-German Affairs, for the impact it will have in the Soviet occupation zone.'[8]

No mention was made yet of the size of their respective contributions, since the cost estimate they had been given was still considered to be too high. Even so, the Federal Ministry of the Interior asked the City of Kassel to make a modest but sufficient sum of money available to the Society to start preparations, while an urgent downward review of the financial estimates was made in Kassel.

A few days later, the project finally began to get off the ground: on January 25, 1955, the Hessian Ministry of Finance certified its financial contribution, which would go towards adapting the Fridericianum Museum, badly destroyed during the war, for use as the exhibition venue. With this confirmation, 'the spatial conditions for the international exhibition *Western Art of the Twentieth Century* should be guaranteed.'[9] More good news came in the days that followed: on January 27 the Federal Ministry of the Interior confirmed its financial support, and on February 3 the Federal Ministry of Pan-German Affairs followed suit with a contribution of the same amount. At last, with just five months to go before the scheduled opening date, the working committee could finally apply themselves to the task at hand.

How much did the 1955 documenta eventually cost and how much did each party pay? After the close of the exhibition – which ended in deficit – the exact figures borne by each administrative body, which had risen with every consecutive review, revealed that some DM 50,000 had come from the City of Kassel and the Hesse region and DM 100,000 from the Federal Ministries of the Interior and Pan-German Affairs.

---

[9] Heinrich Troeger [former Hessian Minister of Finance], letter to the Society for Western Art of the Twentieth Century, January 25, 1955, documenta archiv, AA, d01, 20, fol. 107.

[10] documenta annual accounts, documenta archiv, Kassel.

[11] The term and the concept of 'sponsorship' as we understand them today were not used in documenta until the preparations for documenta 8, in the first half of the 1980s.

[12] See Birgit Joos, Philip Oswalt and Daniel Tyradelles [eds.], 'Die Bauhaus-Idee als Inspirationsquelle für Arnold Bode', in *Bauhaus documenta. Vision und Marke.* Leipzig: Spector Books, 2019.

[13] 'Spenden' [Donations], undated list [1955], documenta archiv, AA, d01, 16, fol. 141.

[14] It was not until documenta 5 in 1972 that the financial management of the exhibitions became professionalised and that the general administration, which until then had been performed by civil servants of the City of Kassel with parallel responsibilities, became a full-time occupation and financial data was recorded with greater precision. Other forms of financial support, including, for example, the funding of the production of works by artists or their galleries, became increasingly common, yet were consistently left out of the global figures. Therefore, the official budget given for each documenta does not necessarily coincide with the actual cost of the exhibition, since the expenses borne by third parties were not factored in.

The official balance sheets kept in the documenta archiv show additional income in the form of 'donations' from companies and private individuals (DM 22,000), ticket sales (DM 93,000) and revenue from the sale of the catalogues and exhibition material after the closure of the exhibition (DM 64,00).[10] In total, the budget for the first edition amounted to DM 379,000, of which 52% came from institutional contributions and 25% from ticket sales. These percentages would remain more or less constant in the following three editions of documenta, with state support decreasing slightly and ticket sales increasing slightly. From documenta 5 onwards, however, public administrations would increase their share and constitute the project's main source of funding, remaining so, with only minor percentage variations, to this day.

Although it was clear to the organisers from the start that the financial burden of the project would necessarily fall on public institutions, the early financial forecasts also included monetary contributions from individuals and private entities, then known as 'donors'.[11] The involvement of these early donors was almost always based around their personal relationships with the organisers. In Bode's case, his extensive network of contacts in industry was hugely helpful in this regard. Among the preparatory documentation concerning the 1955 exhibition are several internal lists of potential 'donors' that include names such as Rasch, a wallpaper company founded at the end of the 19th century in Osnabrück which had already worked with artists from the Bauhaus School on its designs, as well as with Bode himself; the plastics manufacturer Göppinger Kaliko und Kunstleder Werke, with whom Bode had maintained a working relationship since 1951;[12] Sprengel, a chocolate manufacturer in Hanover whose owners were also art collectors; the corporations AEG, Siemens, Vereinigte Grassstoffwerke and Hoesch; the building materials manufacturers Eternit AG in Hamburg and Resopal in Gross-Umstadt, and the paint manufacturer Pelikan.[13]

These companies' contributions would come either in the form of money or, sometimes, in the form of materials, products or manpower. In other words, they were contributions 'in kind'. Over time, as documenta grew and its budget increased, the model of in-kind contributions expanded to cover a wider range of formulae whose economic equivalence was rarely recorded in the organisation's accounts. Until 1972, in fact, the private 'donations' were only vaguely recorded on the balance sheets, and it is not clear what proportion of the event's overall costs was accounted for by in-kind contributions.[14] This is one of the reasons why it is difficult to say with absolute certainty what the real costs of one or other edition

kassel'64

27. Juni - 5. Oktober

documenta III

Internationale Ausstellung   Museum Fridericianum · Alte Galerie · Orangerie · WKS Auepark

4. PRESSE-INFORMATION: Unterstützung der documenta III

Fondation
Européenne
de la Culture

Der Rat der Gouverneure der Europäischen Kulturstiftung (Fondation Européenne de la Culture) mit dem Sitz in Amsterdam hat beschlossen, in Übereinstimmung mit den Zielen der documenta III die Kosten für die Teilausstellung der Handzeichnungen seit 1880 in voller Höhe bis zum Betrag von 80 000 Mark zu übernehmen. - Seine Königliche Hoheit, Prinz Bernhard der Niederlande hat sich in seiner Eigenschaft als Vorsitzender der Kulturstiftung im Grundsätzlichen dazu bereiterklärt, die Ausstellung der Handzeichnungen innerhalb der documenta III mit einer Ansprache in Kassel zu eröffnen.

Die Europäische Kulturstiftung hat es sich zur Aufgabe gemacht, "einerseits die Förderung verschiedener kultureller Aufgaben und Werte in Europa anzuregen und andererseits einen Beitrag zur Schaffung eines europäischen Bewusstseins als 'conditio sine qua non' zur Verwirklichung der europäischen Einheit zu liefern."

International
Council of
Museums

Der internationale Museumsrat (International Council of Museums, abgekürzt ICOM), eine Einrichtung der UNESCO mit dem Sitz in Paris, hat durch seine Kommission für internationale Kunstausstellungen das Patronat für die documenta III übernommen, indem er ihr von drei möglichen Prädikaten ("registrée", "agréée" oder "patronnée") das höchste, nämlich "patronnée", verliehen hat. Dieses Prädikat erleichtert der Ausstellungsleitung der documenta während der Vorbereitungszeit den internationalen Leihverkehr mit Museen in aller Welt (auch im Ostblock) und sichert den Kunstwerken während des Transports nach Kassel bevorzugte Abfertigung durch die Zollbehörden an den Grenzübergängen.

Presse + Information

35 Kassel
Museum Fridericianum
u. Fünffensterstraße 8
Fernruf (0561-Kassel)
7 41 68 u. 19 26 826

Press release in which the organisation of
documenta III confirms the sponsorship agreement
with the European Cultural Foundation, ca. 1964.
Source: documenta archiv, AA, d03, 35, fol. 82.

---

[15] For a detailed history of the Congress's activities, see Frances Stonor Saunders, *Who Paid the Piper? The CIA and the Cultural Cold War.* London: Granta, 1999.

[16] The Congress funded publications with a wide circulation in those years, such as *Der Monat*, launched by Melvin Lasky in West Berlin as early as 1948; *Preuves*, published in Paris in 1951 and edited by François Bondy; *Encounter*, founded by poet Stephen Spender and journalist Irving Kristol in the UK in 1953; and *Cuadernos*, a magazine aimed at Latin American audiences, founded in 1953 in Chile and edited by Spanish journalist Julián Gorkín.

of documenta really were, especially in the early days – a difficulty that is compounded by the fact that the few historical studies published on documenta's financial situation do not always offer matching figures.

Although initially the main benefactors of documenta were private companies in the field of manufacturing and industry, the number of 'donors' soon began to grow and diversify, prompting other entities of a more institutional nature to follow suit. These included embassies, cultural institutes and organisations dedicated to promoting the artistic careers of fellow citizens and the art of their respective countries, and other supranational cultural sponsors which not uncommonly followed political as well as cultural agendas. After all, in the ideological battles of the Cold War, cultural sponsorship was a trump card – and documenta was not always unreceptive to such matters.

In terms of the cultural propaganda strategies in operation since 1950, the relevance of MoMA's International Exhibitions Program is beyond doubt. As part of its efforts to achieve its objectives, the United States government did more than just support the programme: it created a 'tool', called the Congress for Cultural Freedom (CCF) which, while outwardly 'clean' and upfront, was in fact wielded in the shadows by the invisible arm of the Central Intelligence Agency. Officially state-funded by the US government, the Congress also received funds from the Ford Foundation, the Fairbanks Foundation and other American philanthropic entities, which, in turn, received undercover money from the secret services.

The Congress was founded in West Berlin in the summer of 1950 and remained active until 1967, when its main source of funding was publicly revealed, ruining its prestige and hastening its demise.[15] In addition to providing generous financial support to anti-communist cultural initiatives of all kinds, the CCF's principal activity was the propagation of ideas and views through an established network of magazines spread almost all over the world.[16] On a smaller scale, the Congress also organised – or helped to finance – a series of art exhibitions which all shared a common denominator: the notion that artistic modernity was a symbol of innovation, internationalism and freedom, values unequivocally associated with the countries of the Western bloc: 'Temporary, with an emphasis on "new", and often intended to tour afterwards, from 1952 onwards the CCF's exhibitions used communication models, spatial strategies and a conceptual framework to convey the political values of the pre-war avant-garde on a formalist and apolitical historiography of modernity. Framed within the ideological system of capitalism and designed to re-educate the individual away from Nazism and communism, these exhibitions

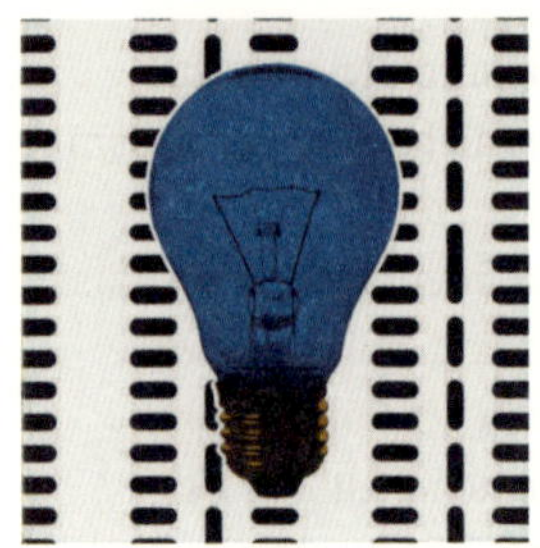

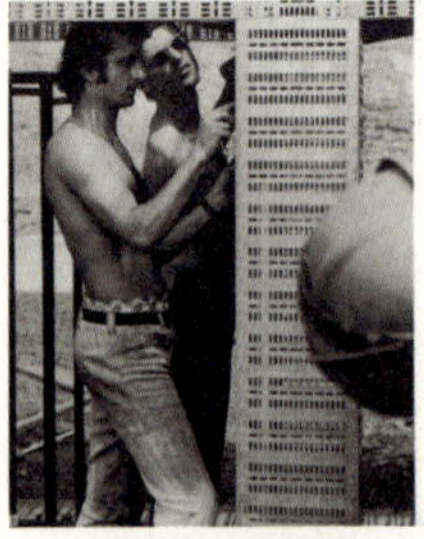

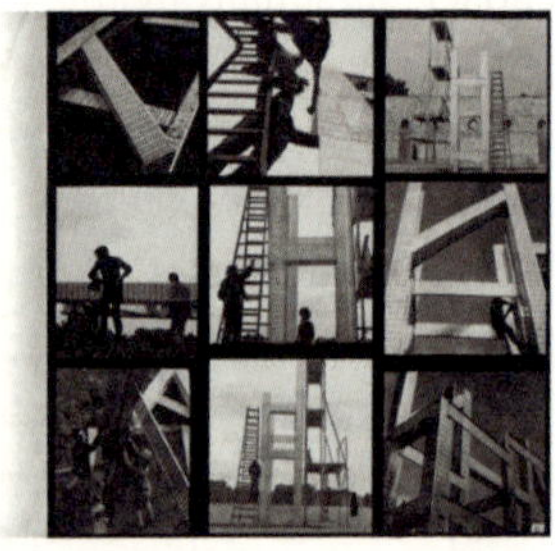

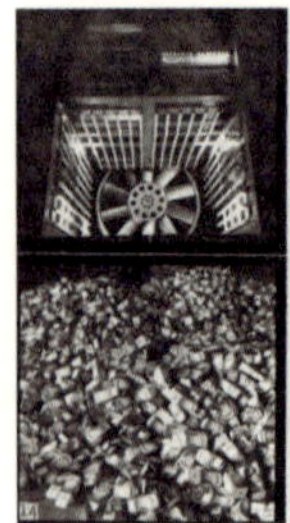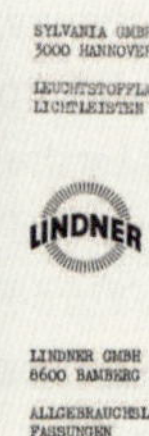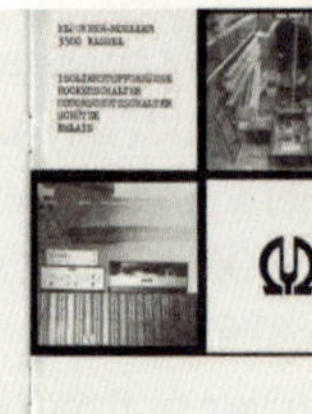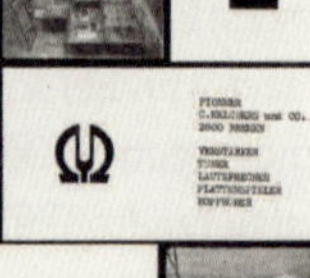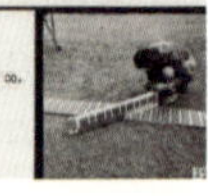

Projekt Geldmacher Mariotti [brochure].
Kassel: self-published, 1968.

17 Paz Guevara, 'Exhibition as a Medium for Geopolitical Operations: Digging Up the Exhibitions of the Congress for Cultural Freedom'. In Anselm Franke, Nida Ghouse, Paz Guevara, and Antonia Majaca [eds.], Parapolitics: Cultural Freedom and the Cold War. Berlin: Haus der Kulturen der Welt and Sternberg Press, 2021, p. 298.

18 *Werner Schmalenbach*. Cologne: Verlag der Buchhandlung Walther König, 2011, p. 45. [Werner Schmalenbach interviewed by Eduard Beaucamp.]

19 Since at least 1954, Barr had been a member of the American Committee for Cultural Freedom [ACCF] section of Congress.

20 Paz Guevara, op. cit., p. 298-299.

21 *Das Ursprüngliche und die Moderne*, exhibition organised by Berliner Festwochen and the Akademie der Künste, August 23 to September 27, 1964.

22 *Afrika: 100 Stämme, 100 Meisterwerke*, School of Fine Arts, Charlottenburg [Berlin], September 12 to October 4, 1964.

23 Rudolf Zwirner with Nicola Kuhn, *Ich wollte immer Gegenwart. Autobiographie.* Cologne: Wienand Verlag, 2019, p. 120.

established the value of "cultural freedom" in opposition to what they called the "directed culture" of the Soviet bloc, of which socialist realism and political muralism were examples.'[17]

Clearly, the historical-political perspectives of documenta's organisers dovetailed neatly with this ideological scenario and collaborations were soon formalised. In 1959, when documenta exhibited in Europe for the first time a selection of American Abstract Expressionist paintings chosen personally by the 'curator-cum-secret agent'[18] Porter McCray, part of the expense of shipping the works to Kassel was borne by MoMA's International Exhibitions Program, whose director, Alfred H. Barr, was a member of the US branch of the Congress for Cultural Freedom.[19] Indeed, a number of other personal connections were established between Congress members and the organisers of the first editions of documenta: Will Grohmann, who was part of the Kassel organising team until the third edition, participated in a symposium organised by the Congress in 1960 in West Berlin, as did Werner Haftmann.[20] Likewise, in 1964, as part of the cultural festival mounted in Berlin by Nicolas Navokov, Secretary General of the Congress, Grohmann helped with the exhibition *The Original and the Moderns*[21] on display at the Berlin Academy of Arts, while Arnold Bode was commissioned to design the exhibition *Africa: 100 Tribes, 100 Masterpieces*[22] for the Berlin School of Fine Arts.

In addition to these connections, funds from the Congress for Cultural Freedom found their way into the documenta's coffers on at least one occasion. In 1964, shortly before opening, documenta III was happily announcing the Amsterdam-based Fondation Européenne de la Culture (FEC)'s release of DM 80,000 to cover the entire cost of the exhibition's drawing section, brokered by German businessman Gustav Stein, one of the first private collectors to make a firm commitment to contemporary art in West Germany.[23] At the time, Stein was both vice-chairman of the FEC and a member of the documenta Board, a supervisory body in place since the second edition. Not long after, in 1967, the instrumental role of the FEC – which turned out to be one of the Congress for Cultural Freedom's main channels of allocation of CIA funds to different European cultural projects – was laid bare when the press revealed the close ties between the CIA and the Congress for Cultural Freedom.

This scoop has gone down in the annals of documenta's history as scarcely more than an anecdote – and the same goes for other circumstances or incidents relating to the financial side of things. Even though documenta's financial antics and status have often been the subject of commentary, intense debate and even angry polemic in German media, especially when airing the deficits that the project has regularly incurred throughout its existence, the exhibition's financial strengths and weaknesses have rarely been discussed or studied, with historians preferring to focus on art proposals, currents and trends, curatorial styles and their aesthetic and political contexts. Indeed, attempts to reflect on the connection between money and artistic production around documenta have tended to come from artists, who have addressed this issue through their artistic work. One early example of this critical attitude to documenta's funding strategy is the large-scale installation *Projekt Geldmacher Mariotti*, presented in 1968 in the Orangerie park, which highlighted the relevance that 'contributions in kind' from business had reached at the time, while seeking to ignite a discussion around these issues in the public domain.

In the spring of 1968, artists Klaus Geldmacher and Francesco Mariotti, both recent graduates of the Hamburg School of Fine Arts (whose director was Herbert von Buttlar, a member of the documenta organising team) were invited to create a project for the *Ambiente* section of documenta IV.[24] Entitled simply *Projekt Geldmacher Mariotti*, their proposal consisted of a gigantic wooden and metal cube in the open air fitted with a propeller, a wiring system and some 10,000 different coloured light bulbs. 'This object could be presented – just as it is now – as a charming work of art with sounds and music and fascinating light effects, and it would probably be quite well received,'[25] the artists stated in the small publication that was brought out to accompany the work. But, as they went on to say, their intention was not aesthetic, but political. With their large mechanical sculpture in the Orangerie they sought to open up a space for dialogue through a 'photoacoustic experience': 'We have been given a forum which allows us to start a discussion' and which should fulfil a 'function as a medium for communication and a space to discuss future definitions of art'.[26]

As would often be the case in the early editions of documenta, the production schedule for *Projekt Geldmacher Mariotti* was so tight that

---

[24] The *Ambiente* section was financed by the documenta foundation, whose history is described in the following chapters of this book.

[25] Klaus Geldmacher and Francesco Mariotti, *Projekt Geldmacher Mariotti – 4. Documenta* [brochure]. Kassel: self-published, 1968.

[26] Klaus Geldmacher and Francesco Mariotti, ibid.

[27] Willi Bongard, 'Markt für 100 Tage'. In *Die Zeit* no. 29, July 19, 1968, p. 27 (monthly section 'Art Market'). In addition to editing this section and contributing regularly to *Die Zeit*, Willi Bongard was one of the three curators invited to select projects for *Ambiente* at documenta IV.

[28] Klaus Geldmacher and Francesco Mariotti, op. cit.

finalising the installation in time for the opening of the exhibition was nothing short of miraculous. The budget had not been approved until May, and then, as work began, the two artists quickly realised that their estimated costs of around DM 17,000 were far from realistic. A new calculation showed that the final cost would be more than double. To solve the problem, they immediately contacted some 150 industrial suppliers, whom they had selected after a quick visit to the Hanover Industrial Fair which had just taken place, and asked if they would be so kind as to provide the materials they needed to make their gigantic light cube a reality.

They did not have to wait long for the responses. In the end, of the thirty companies expressing a willingness to collaborate, only about fifteen came forward with the materials, most of which were loaned: 'Bayer Farbenfabriken donated 105 Makrolon plastic sheets at the value of DM 10,000. Bettermann-Electro cHG lent 952 metres of track cable, and Fr. Jorns Kupferwerk lent a large axial fan worth DM 8,000. The companies Pioneer C. Melchers & Co (an amplification system) and Klöckner-Moeller-Werke (distributors and circuits) also lent material. Discounts of 50% were given by Lindner GmbH for 9,000 incandescent lamps and Sylvania GmbH for 100 fluorescent lamps.'[27]

The 20-page brochure accompanying *Projekt Geldmacher Mariotti* shared not only details of this sort, but also a detailed breakdown of the costs and an account of the various obstacles the funding had encountered along the way. It also reserved plenty of space for the sponsoring companies to sport their logos alongside photographs taken of the piece as it was assembled. Furthermore, it included a text by the artists in which they asked Bode to explain his understanding of the concept of 'artistic freedom' which, after all, had been one of the main motivations for setting up documenta. Geldmacher and Mariotti expressed their view that with this, the fourth edition of the exhibition, such a concept might now be considered amortised and questioned what the essence of artistic freedom might be now, given the public administration's role in ensuring the economic viability of documenta: 'We need to investigate how the State guarantees artistic freedom in this context, what motivates it, whether liberal insecurity, tolerant negligence, respect for a minority, a deliberate desire to deceive the public or a vision anchored in certain political-cultural contexts...'[28]

In line with the protests calling for a total shake-up of institutional authority of all kinds – let's not forget this was 1968 – Geldmacher and Mariotti's piece served to spotlight what the impact and the consequences of institutional funding might be on an event like documenta. Merely attempting to address this issue so explicitly was in itself a bold and

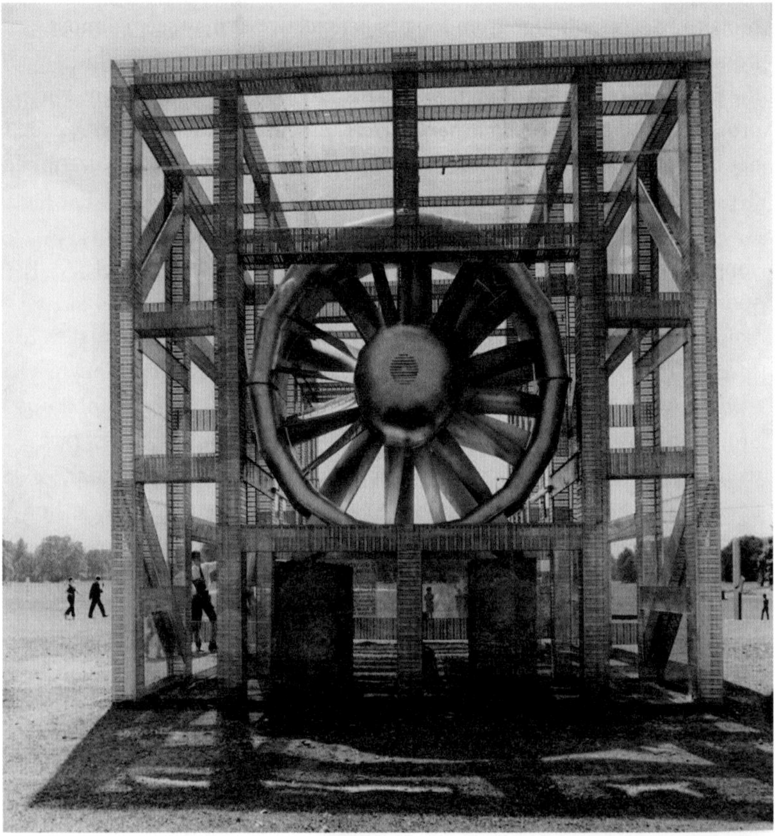

Klaus Geldmacher and Francesco
Mariotti. *Projekt Geldmacher Mariotti*,
documenta IV, Kassel, 1968.
Photo: documenta archiv.

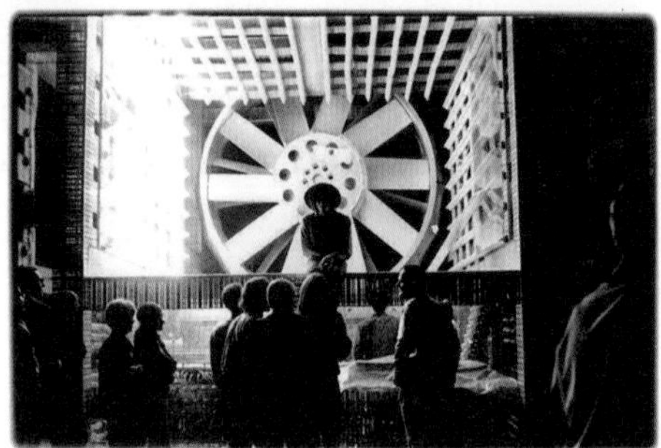

29 As the surviving correspondence from the documenta foundation shows, after the end of documenta IV, rather than profit, the gigantic piece had generated a whole new financial problem due to its elevated storage costs, even though it had been partially dismantled so that the technical equipment loaned by the various private sponsors could be returned.

provocative act, although from today's perspective, it may seem almost ironic that the artists were questioning public financial support while the private sponsoring for their piece failed to arouse any suspicion. The problem that *Projekt Geldmacher Mariotti* essentially addresses, however, is not institutional support per se, but more generally the inevitable economic dependence implicit in artistic production.

Apart from probing Bode about the symbolic price of institutional support from the pages of a brochure displaying corporate logos of sponsoring companies so big they could be mistaken for illustrations, Geldmacher and Mariotti also set out to examine other practices that were characteristic of mercantile and commercial relations generally. They devised two new tactics intended to help cover the costs of their ambitious project: on the one hand, a complex system of allocation of 'shares' that would hypothetically yield 'investors' a profit of DM 500 each if, after documenta, they succeeded in finding a buyer for their outdoor piece; and on the other, in the manner of a duchampian *Boîte en valise* edition, the commercialisation of a limited run of 'scale reproductions' (30 x 30 x 20 cm approx.) of their great cube of lights.

No evidence has been found suggesting that *Projekt Geldmacher Mariotti* was sold after documenta closed,[29] and so one can assume that the shares system the pair devised did not work as expected in terms of profits. As for the limited edition, by commercialising it, Geldmacher and Mariotti were in fact resorting to the classic fundraising method used in art: the sale of works. The formula was by no means exceptional. The documenta organisers had employed it themselves to raise funds via an entity specifically created for the purpose – the documenta foundation – which, thanks to revenue from previous editions, had, by 1968, enough money to pay not only for half of the cost of *Projekt Geldmacher Mariotti,* but for the entire *Ambiente* section.

Idealism vs business sense, or exhibiting vs selling

[1] Scott Reyburn, 'At Venice Biennale, the
Art's for Sale, if You Know the Right People'.
In *The New York Times*, May 14, 2019.

[2] Ines Schlenker, 'Defining National Socialist Art:
The First Grosse Deutsche Kunstausstellung
in 1937'. In Olaf Peters [ed.], op. cit., p. 92.

Not long ago, the *New York Times* ran a piece on the opening of the 58th edition of the Venice Biennale, the oldest and most venerable of all the regular events devoted to the visual arts, which addressed the difficult relationship that major publicly funded exhibitions and the art market have today. The Biennale, the piece argued, 'epitomises the level of conflict in today's art world when it comes to questions of money. For some, particularly in officialdom, *la Biennale* should have the commerce-free purity of a museum. [...] For others, the event is also the world's biggest art fair, if you just know whom and how to ask.'[1] The expression 'commerce-free purity' aptly sums up, without room for too much nuance, the attitude expected today of a museum, especially if it is state-owned, and, by extension, of events defrayed by the public purse such as many biennials or documenta itself. Such purity requires forgoing any hint of interaction with the art market and keeping as far away as possible any strategies or manoeuvres connected to sales that may affect the exhibition and acquisition of art works and the professional careers of their authors.

Leaving aside the fact that purity is an ideal and hardly transferable to real world contingencies, and bearing in mind that such qualms appear not to affect merchandising, space rental and other commercial schemes that public and private museums consistently deploy to offset 'incredibly dwindling' budgets, it is only recently that the tension between market and exhibition has been seen as a source of conflict. In the universal exhibitions of the nineteenth century, buying and selling (although not necessarily art) were common practice, and continued to be in the first half of the twentieth century at shows like the *Great German Art Exhibition* of 1937, which, 'apart from its value as propaganda, was primarily and above all a very successful commercial event, attracting a very large number of visitors and obtaining outstanding sales figures'.[2] In the field of art, the line between non-lucrative activities and commerce remained blurred well into in the second half of the twentieth century. Even the Venice Biennale kept its sales office open until 1968, and the commercialisation of art works (in addition to tickets and catalogues) to obtain income was a strategy the promoters of the early documentas were also more than willing to use: in the first documenta, the loan conditions established a 15% commission on the sale price of each work of art sold during the exhibition. The commission rose to 20% in 1968 and continued to feature in loan contracts until documenta 8, in 1987.

That the promoters of the first documentas explicitly determined such a commission reflects the ease with which they regarded sales as an integral part of every exhibition. This view, in fact, was not uncommon in 1950s Germany, as is borne out by other testimonies, such as Werner

SCHWAN & BÖGER G.M.B.H. · DÜSSELDORF

BUCH- UND KUNSTHANDLUNG · ANTIQUARIAT · DÜSSELDORF
KÖNIGSALLEE 14-16 · EINGANG SCHADOWSTRASSE · RUF 13638
Bank: Bankverein Westdeutschland, Düsseldorf · Postscheckkonto Essen Nr. 870

Düsseldorf, 2. Juni 1955.

E i n s c h r e i b e n

DOKUMENTA
Sekretariat

K a s s e l
Landesmuseum

Verkäuflich

Zur Ansicht !

1	Aquatinta PABLO PICASSO " Torse de femme "	DM	800.-
1	Lithographie PABLO PICASSO " La mère et les enfants "	DM	450.-
1	Lithographie MARINO MARINI " Pferd auf rotem Grund "	DM	230.-

Diese Blätter sind bisher unveröffentlicht.
Die Picasso Blätter waren auch noch nicht
in der Züricher Ausstellung vertreten, da
erst später erschienen.

Bö

Note from the Schwan & Böger gallery, Düsseldorf,
certifying the delivery of prints by Pablo Picasso and
Marino Marini to the organisers of documenta, 1955.
In red, handwritten, the indication *Verkäuflich* ['For sale'].
Source: documenta archiv, AA, d01, 17, fol. 59.

[3] *Werner Schmalenbach*, op. cit., p. 33.

[4] There are also Kunstvereine in Austria,
Switzerland and northern Italy, but it is in
Germany where this institutional model
is most established and widespread.

[5] Bettina Steinbrügge quoted in Veronika Beck
and Miriam Michalski, 'Demokratisierung der
Kunst. Geschichte der Hamburger Jahresgaben'.
In Uwe Fleckner and Uwe M. Schneede (eds.),
*Bürgerliche Avantgarde. 200 Jahre Kunstverein
Hamburg*. Berlin: Hatje Cantz, 2017, p. 94.

Schmalenbach's. In 1957, during his tenure as director of the Kestner Gesellschaft in Hanover, he celebrated the commercial success of a large display of Schwitters collages in which the institution 'charged a 15% commission on each sale. I sold Schwitters collages every day. I had to send for supplies to Oslo. For the first time since its foundation in 1906, the Kestner Gesellschaft was cashing in. When I first arrived in Hanover there was a huge mountain of debt. Suddenly it disappeared'.[3] Certainly, the Kestner Gesellschaft is not a public museum in the strict sense, but an example of a German type of art institution[4] that has included sales in its programme of activities almost from its inception: the *Kunstverein*.

The first Kunstverein, a word that loosely translates as an 'association of people interested in art', was founded in Hamburg in 1817, spawning a string of similar associations in other German cities in the 1820s and 1830s. Made up of a flourishing bourgeoisie, these associations shared the same goal, which was to create an art institution independent of the Church and the nobility, which traditionally had had the power to commission, collect and exhibit works of art. Moreover, they took on the pedagogical task of kindling interest in art and established channels of support for artists who had been left without patronage in the new social order that had emerged out of the French Revolution and the Enlightenment. To raise funds for their activities, the Kunstvereine made the works shown at their exhibitions available for sale, and this was quickly followed by annual raffles of prints and the sale of editions and serial works among members. A somewhat ambivalent space was thus emerging which the Kunstvereine embraced: a space halfway between a private, professional gainful business and a non-profit public institution.

In Germany, the Kunstvereine played a fundamental role in the constitution of a network of spaces dedicated to art in the modern era, promoting as they did the creation of museums wherever there were neither collections belonging to the nobility nor significant private collections. However, democratising access to the fine arts and disseminating the artistic tradition were not the only reasons why their sales were successful. Also at play, albeit implicitly, was the petty-bourgeois ambition to be assimilated into the cultured and powerful social class that engaged in collecting, for whom works of art were a badge of originality and style: it was 'about showing one's own culture, [...] about showing one's own individual identity to the outside world'.[5]

Ironically, this desire for distinction would weigh heavily on the Kunstvereine when, in the second half of the nineteenth century, their editions began to lose value in favour of 'original' artworks, since their

Die Zeit, August 16, 1968, monthly section devoted to information about the art market edited by Willi Bongard.
Source: *Die Zeit* Archive, Hamburg.

[6] Veronika Beck and Miriam Michalski, op. cit., p. 94.

[7] Daniel Henry Kahnweiler died in Paris in 1979, aged 94.

[8] Rolf-Gunter Dienst, 'Interview mit Hein Stünke'. In *Das Kunstwerk. Zeitschrift für bildende Kunst*, no. 6 - XXV, November 1972, p. 9.

[9] Günter Herzog, 'Kunstmarkt 68'. In Zentralarchiv für Deutsche und Internationale Kunstmarktforschung – ZADIK (ed.), *Art Cologne: Die Erste aller Kunstmessen / The First Art Fair*. Cologne: ZADIK and Verlag der Buchhandlung Walther König, 2016, p. 41.

[10] *Freie Internationale Universität*, or FIU for short.

democratising ubiquity had diminished their aura of prestige: 'In our modern society, uniqueness seems to be the measure of all things within the elites, and this must also be reflected in art.'[6] As a result, the popularity of the Kunstvereine declined in the second half of the nineteenth century and the first decades of the twentieth.

The trading activity of the Kunstvereine would rekindle after the Second World War following their shift of focus onto the publication of works solely by living artists. But by then, shortly before the launch of documenta in 1955, the art market had embarked on a profound metamorphosis. Until then, sales had been handled by art dealers – highly cultured and well-connected individuals with a strong personality, who established close personal relationships with artists, provided them with all kinds of support and often steered their careers with a firm hand. But almost all of the most successful dealers of the previous generation, born around 1870-1880 (many of Jewish descent, whose businesses had been ruthlessly persecuted by the Nazis) had died before the war started: Paul Cassirer took his own life in 1926 over a broken heart, Alfred Fechtheim died a pauper in exile in London in 1937, Ambroise Vollard died in 1939 in a traffic accident... Daniel Henry Kahnweiler was almost the only one of the *marchands d'art* of the first half of the century who remained active after the war.[7] When the figure of the art dealer went into decline, the role was taken over by art galleries, which tended to be more professionalised and complex commercial structures than the one-man initiatives of the previous period. Such a development proved unstoppable, even if the still active art dealers watched on in horror, as reflected by the remark Kahnweiler is purported to have made: 'Now there is an art fair in Cologne. Art is moving to the market. It's a mess.'[8]

Amid this transformation, professionalising the market and managing art sales using scientific methods based on quantifiable data were driving some of the initiatives that emerged in the 1960s – initiatives that reflected the growing interest in the matter. One person who paid particular attention to this was Willi Bongard, a journalist specialising in contemporary art and finance who, for a time, was editor of the business section of the weekly *Die Zeit*. In 1965, Bongard began to write about business opportunities in art, and from 1968 ran a monthly page dedicated to the art market, the first of its kind in German media.[9] At the same time, he nurtured close ties with the German art scene, becoming a member of one of the preparatory working committees for documenta IV in 1968, and, along with Klaus Staeck and Georg Meistermann, cooperated with Joseph Beuys in the founding of the Free International University in 1973,[10] where he would

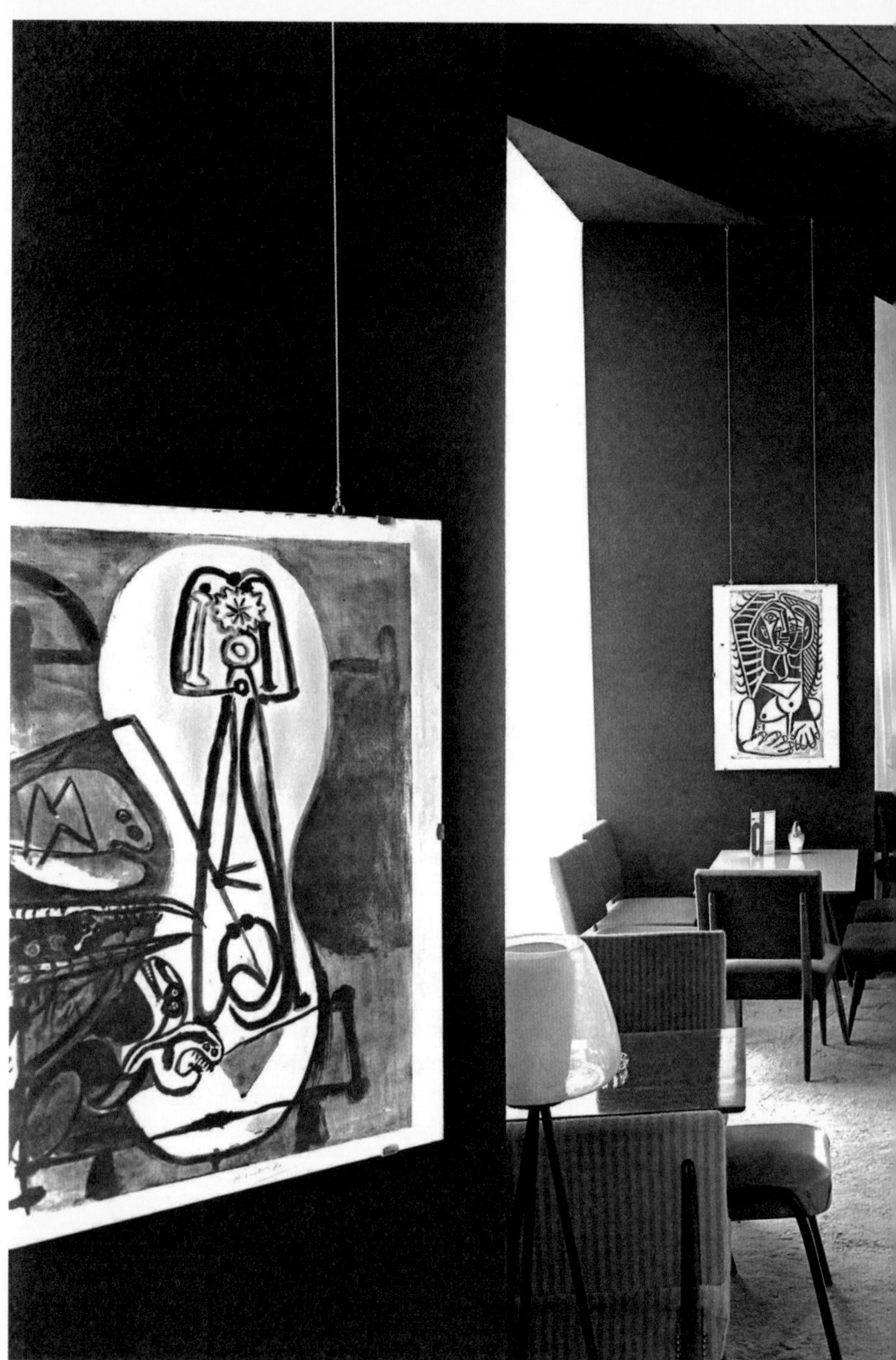

documenta cafeteria, 1955, decorated with prints by Picasso (*Hommards et poissons*, 1949, and *Torse de femme (l'Egyptienne)]*, 1953) and Marino Marini (*Cavalier et chevaux, bordure verte*, 1955). Photo: documenta archiv.

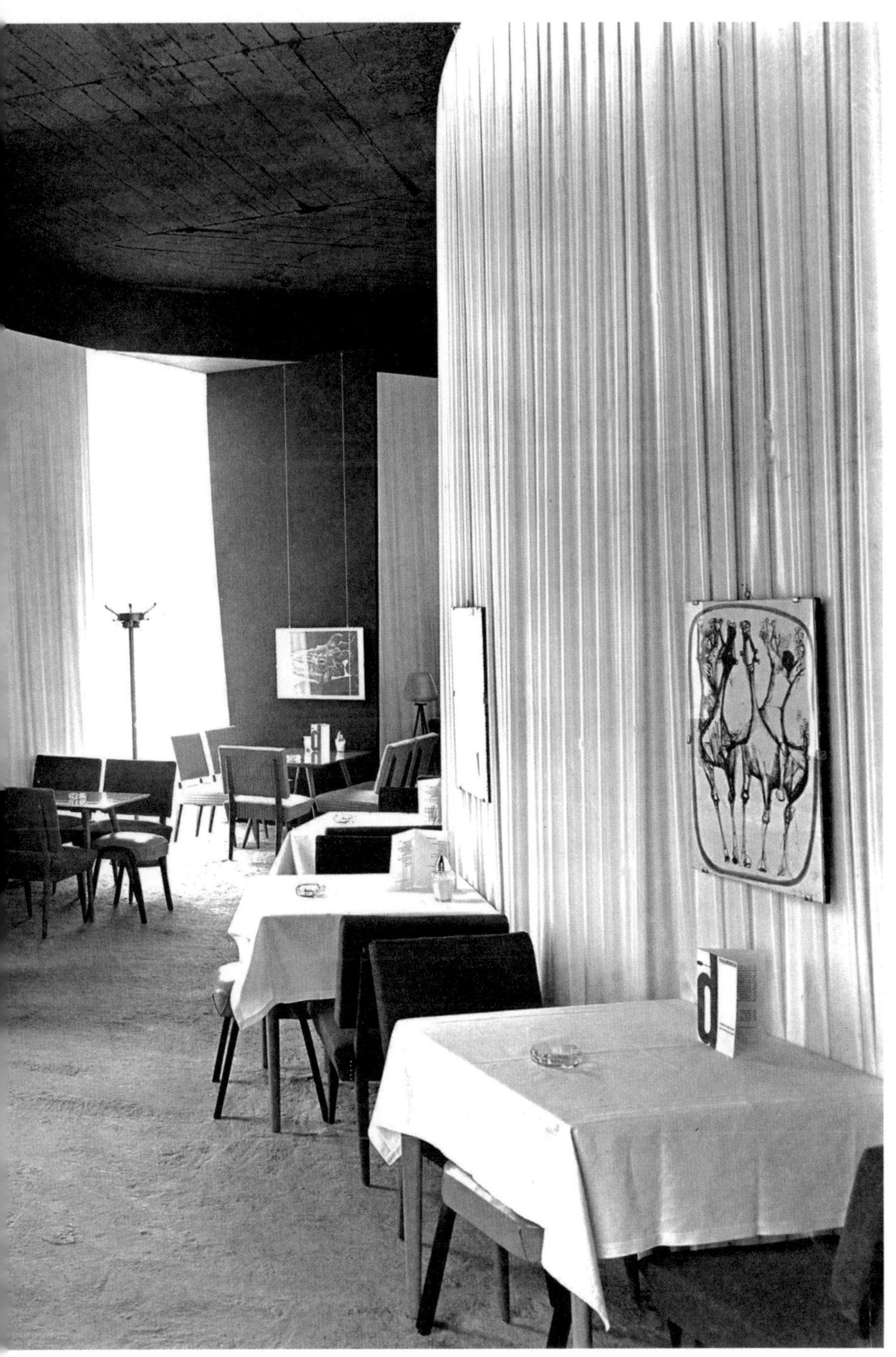

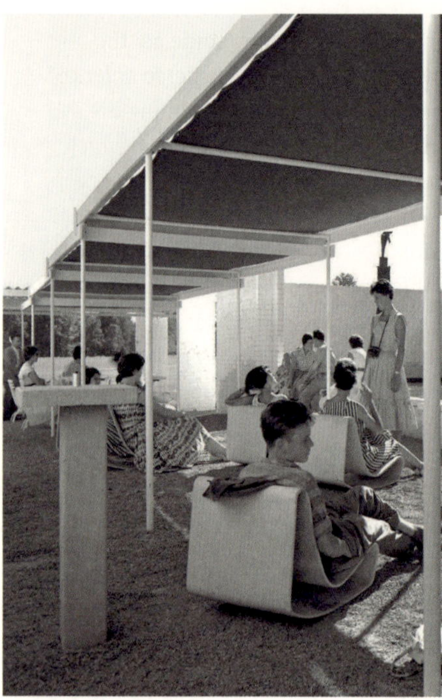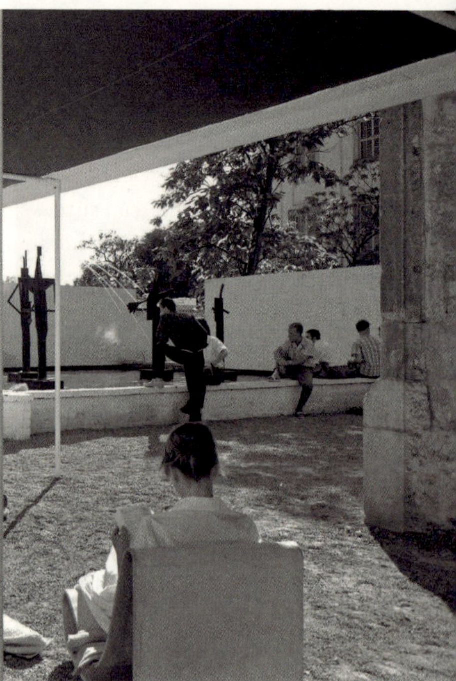

Orangerie gardens during documenta II.
Photo: Günther Becker / documenta archiv.

11 Karl Oskar Blase, introduction to a video
interview with Willi Bongard in the context
of documenta 5, Kassel, 1972. ZKM -
Center for Art and Media Karlsruhe, Archive
Audiovisual documentation of documenta 5.

12 Willi Bongard, *Kunst und Kommerz:
zwischen Passion und Spekulation.*
Oldenburg: Stalling Verlag, 1967.

13 Wieland Schmied, then director of the Kerstner-
Gessellschaft in Hanover, wrote: 'The thesis that
[Bongard] puts forward, according to which
in no other field as in the sale of modern art
is there "so much idealism combined with so
little business sense", is doubly true: because
it is generally true, and also because it is not
often heard. However, his reflections on the
modernisation of the business of art sales
come across as rather provincial.' Wieland
Schmied, 'Kunst & Kommerz. Staunend auf
dem Markt'. In *Der Spiegel,* March 17, 1968.

14 Willi Bongard, *Kunstkompass* 1970, p. 3. See
also Paul Buckermann, *Die Vermessung der
Kunstwelt. Quantifizierende Beobachtungen
und plurale Ordnungen der Kunst.*
Weilerswist: Velbrück Wissenschaft, 2020.

15 *Kunstkompass* 1970, p. 147.

16 Gisela Fehrlin, 'Kasseler Kunst-Messe,
1959'. In *Deutsche Rundschau,*
Baden-Baden, December 1959.

hold a prominent role until his death in 1985. Dubbed by some as 'the unpleasant guardian angel of gallery owners' because of his fierce defence of the art market,[11] in 1967 Bongard published an essay[12] outlining his ideas for professionalising the art business and modernising sales, which centred around his conviction that editions, multiples and serial objects were the key to commercial success. Although his proposals were met with considerable scepticism in the industry,[13] Bongard developed them further, and in 1970 reframed them in his most enduring project: the *Kunstkompass,* or 'Art Compass'.

Published uninterruptedly since its launch, the Kunstkompass is an annual ranking that aims to identify the 100 most influential artists at any given time. The list is compiled by counting the number of solo exhibitions an artist has had in over 200 internationally relevant museums and art centres, the number of times they have participated in more than a hundred group exhibitions (including the Venice Biennale and documenta), and how many reviews in the specialised press and acquisitions by major museums they have had. When it was launched, the Kunstkompass was touted as a 'ranking scale'[14] that could objectively identify the most prestigious artists and thereby reduce the 'uncertainty around the value of art today'.[15] Bongard's intention via this method was to establish an objective evaluation system that measured artists' renown – and consequent economic worth. However, a quick glance is enough to notice the many cracks through which subjectivity creeps into this scale. One such 'crack' is the geographical location of the markers scrutinised: information is gathered overwhelmingly from Germany, the United States, and Northwestern Europe – and some Italian media – and so it should come as no surprise that the artists the Kunstkompass ranks highest tend to come from these areas and in this order.

Bongard's passionate defence of the art market in the 1960s and 1970s was far from commonly accepted, however. In 1959, Gisela Fehrlin, a journalist and editor of the Swiss magazine *Speculum Artis,* lamented in her review of documenta II that 'Today, art is a commodity like nylon clothing and refrigerators. Significantly, the art market employs the same terms to describe its business as are commonly used in the language of commerce (*demand, satisfaction of needs,* etc.), and the attitude is also that of businessmen, who think less about quality and more about success, i.e. revenue.'[16] For Fehrlin, documenta II's only merit was that it united a significant number of works that demonstrated the extent to which art had become vulgarised and meaningless. And the gallery owners were to blame for such decadence: 'The global nebulisation of taste would never

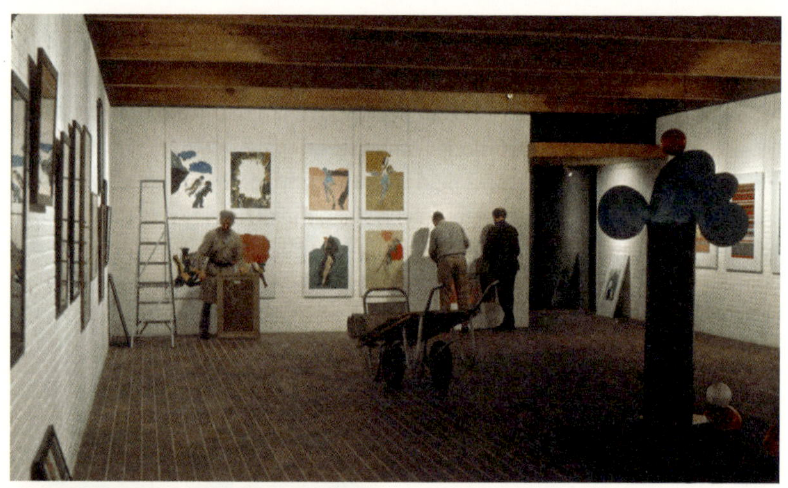

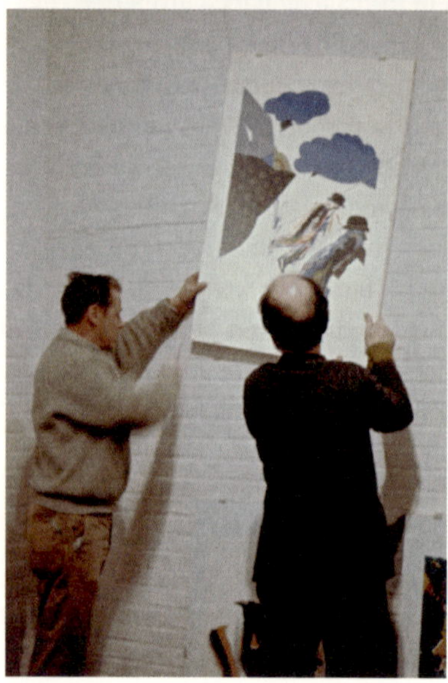

Installation of the exhibition *Værker fra documenta. Grafik og multikunst* in the Louisiana Museum of Modern Art, Humblebæck, 1968.
In the foreground, prints by Allen Jones.
Photo: Louisiana Museum of Modern Art Archive.

[17] Ibid.

[18] Arnold Bode in an anonymous interview, sound recording, c. 1964, documenta archiv (3002490_DIGdA_2_09).

[19] Ibid.

[20] Knud W. Jensen, *Mein Louisiana Leben. Werdegang eines Museums.* Klagenfurt: Ritter Verlag, 1991, p. 39.

have unfolded to such an extent had it not been for the ruthless but lucrative dictatorship of the gallerists. [...] And who buys art today? First of all, the nouveau riche; it used to be a question of education, today it is exclusively a question of money, and the cultivated people in our time are, as experience shows, among the financially worst off. The others are swimming in abundance and are always looking for new ways to grow their profits; since they usually have neither education nor tradition, they cannot know what art is; they are therefore dependent on the art dealer and dutifully acquire what is fashionable.'[17]

How was this seen in Kassel? The connection between art and the art market was a subject the organisers of the first documentas were not keen to discuss. The few surviving records on the matter show their reluctance to explicitly endorse the symbiosis of exhibition and market; but neither could they declare themselves opposed to the sale of works, given that they had had the idea in the first place as a way of boosting their income (or at least avoiding a deficit). In an audio interview held shortly after documenta III, when asked whether the exhibition had 'a certain influence on the way galleries sell', Arnold Bode replied: 'Yes, we have had great success with the sales. [...] Quite surprisingly, it has become apparent that even documenta has become a major art market.'[18] 'Do you think, Mr. Bode, that it is a good thing that documenta has *also become* an art fair?', the interviewer insisted, to which Bode, clearly uncomfortable, answered evasively, 'Yes... It's difficult to say now, because it has come upon us, we can't change it, we can't stop it, we can't... Above all, we can't... Why should we regret it? Basically, there are two aspects: we didn't want the crowds that have crushed us in recent days. Nor, in that sense, did we want the art fair. But it's clear that this documenta enterprise in Central Europe – let's call it Central Europe – probably makes sense. And I think the great charisma of documenta makes sense, because I deeply believe that it is more than just an exhibition in the classical sense, because otherwise people wouldn't have come...'[19]

Certainly, documenta quickly became 'more than just an exhibition in the classical sense', and its impact on visitors was felt right from the start, and in some cases, it was truly profound. The reaction to documenta II of Knut Jensen, founder and director of the Louisiana Museum of Art in Humblebæck, just outside Copenhagen, illustrates to what extent.

Jensen first visited documenta in 1959, barely a year after inaugurating the Louisiana Museum of Modern Art which housed an exhibition of his own private collection of almost solely Danish art from the early modern period. As he later acknowledged, that visit to Kassel would be 'the greatest shock that art would ever cause in [my] life'.[20] The impressive selection

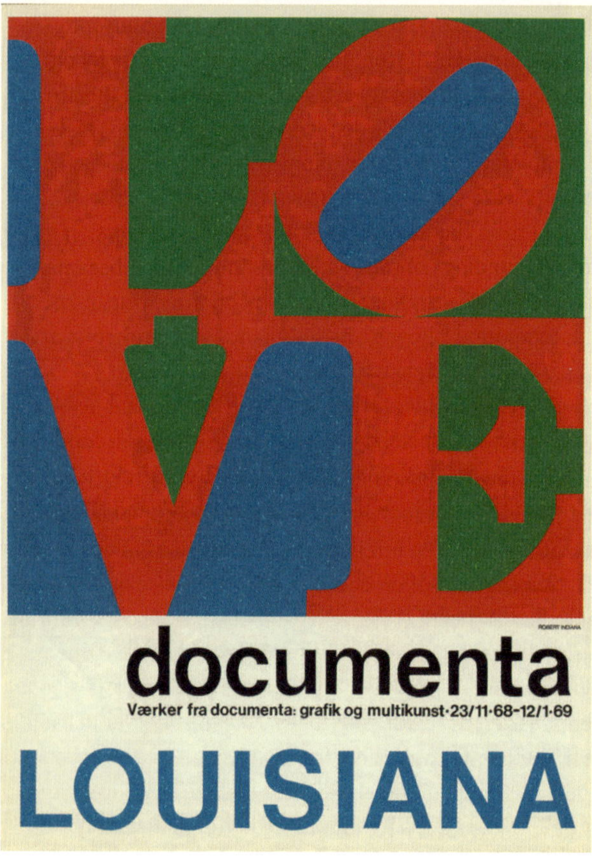

Exhibition poster for *Værker fra documenta.*
Grafik og multikunst, 1968, illustrated with
Love, by Robert Indiana.
Photo: Louisiana Museum of Modern Art Archive.

21 Kristian Handberg, 'The Shock of the
Contemporary: documenta II and the
Louisiana Museum'. In *On Curating*, no. 33.
[https://www.on-curating.org/issue-33-
reader/the-shock-of-the-contemporary-
documenta-ii-and-the-louisiana-museum.
html#_edn9, retrieved in January 2022]

22 *Værker fra documenta. Udstilling på
Lou[i]siana 1959,* Louisiana Museum of
Art, October 20 to November 3, 1959.

23 *Værker fra documenta. Grafik og multikunst,
1968,* Louisiana Museum of Art, November
23, 1968, to January 12, 1969.

24 Moreover, only part of them – the work of thirty-
four artists out of a total of fifty-eight – had
been published by the documenta foundation.

of art works he saw in Kassel marked a turning point in his philosophy
regarding his own collection, which from then on would move its focus
to international (Western) contemporary art. And it was not just the art
he found impressive; it was also Bode's display. In Kassel, Jensen was
confronted with a completely original way of understanding exhibition
design by which visitors were engaged in a new and intensive experience,
one in which art flowed from thè exhibition halls into the corridors, gardens,
cafeteria and entire surroundings of the exhibition. In Kassel, it became
clear to Jensen that a new museum 'had to be based on three principles:
representing the contemporary, showing its foundations in modernist art
history, and creating a total experience for the viewers'.[21]

Such was Jensen's excitement at what he saw in Kassel that he
succeeded in persuading the organisers of the event to send a selection
of the exhibits to the Louisiana Museum immediately after the close of
documenta II. The presentation, which took place in October and November
1959,[22] was the first of only two occasions when documenta organised
anything close to a 'tour', and the second would also come about under Knut
Jansen's instigation. In 1968, after a visit to documenta IV, Jensen reprised
his idea of showing a selection of works from Kassel at the Louisiana
Museum. However, for logistical reasons, the idea was superseded by
another, more practicable plan, which was to show a selection of the prints
exhibited in the graphic art section at documenta. To this end, contacts
were quickly established with the various galleries that had supplied work
to Kassel: Editions Alecto and Kasmin Gallery in London, Denise René in
Paris, Marlborough Gallery in London and New York, Multiples, Inc in New
York and, in Germany, Edition Domberger, Galerie Neuendorf, Galerie Nicke
and, of course, Galerie Der Spiegel and Galerie Rudolf Zwirner. Jensen also
contacted the Museum of Modern Art, which provided a complete series of
prints by Jasper Johns, who ended up having the largest number of works on
show at the Louisiana Museum.

The list of works and their sale prices that featured in the exhibition
brochure[23] produced for the occasion reveals that not all the prints
exhibited in Louisiana Museum had previously been on view in Kassel.[24]
Rather, the idea had primarily been to replicate, through graphic work, the
overwhelming American presence felt at documenta IV. Accordingly, the list
of artists included names like Jim Dine, Robert Indiana, Jasper Johns, Allen
Jones, Ellsworth Kelly, Roy Lichtenstein, Louise Nevelson, Kenneth Noland,
Robert Rauschenberg, Martial Raysse, Larry Rivers, James Rosenquist,
George Segal, Tony Smith, Frank Stella and Tom Weselmann. Perhaps the
only surprise in the selection of artists was the inclusion of Dieter Roth

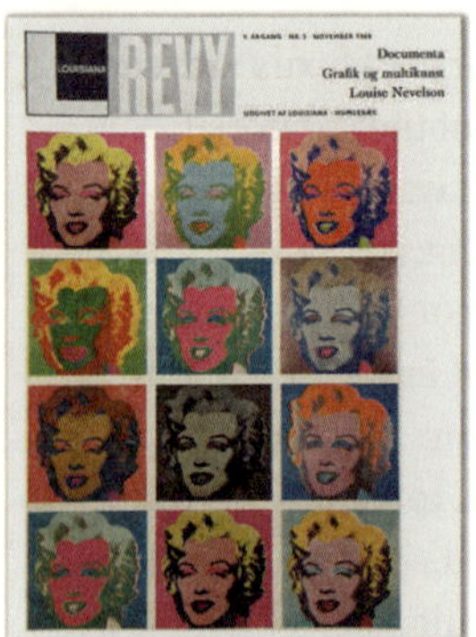

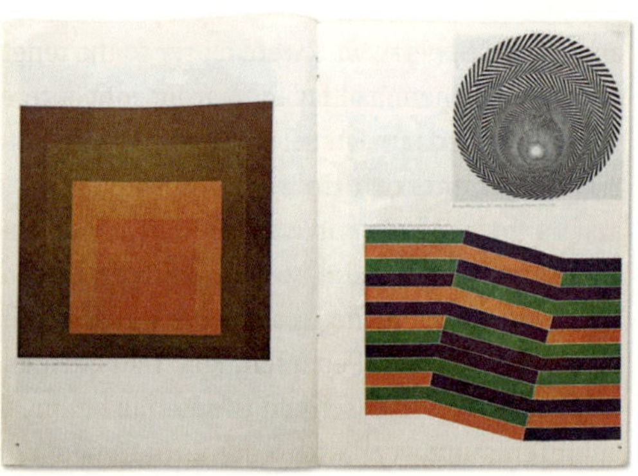

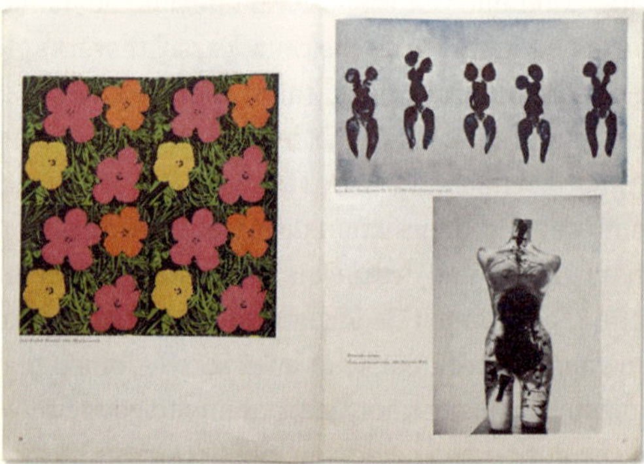

Louisiana Revy, Louisiana Museum of Modern
Art, November 1968: cover and section
devoted to the exhibition of prints *Værker fra
documenta. Grafik og multikunst.*

25 F. W. Øberg-Pedersen [head of the Ars Studeo
gallery in Aarhus at the time], letter to Knud
Jensen, May 29, 1969, Archive of the Louisiana
Museum of Modern Art, Humblebæck.

and Daniel Spoerri, who were closer to the tenets of the Fluxus movement which, until then, had failed to arouse the interest of the curatorial committee in charge of selecting graphic art for documenta.

The prints on display in Louisiana were, of course, put up for sale, just as they had been in Kassel – how could they not? But the exhibition's commercial results did not live up to expectations. In a letter sent to Knud Jensen following the closure of the exhibition, Aarhus gallery owner F. W. Øberg-Pedersen, who had been asked to help with the logistics of sales, described the idea of selling prints of the exhibition as 'an interesting work with a somewhat meagre result'. He complained that the prices had been too high and had put off potential buyers, advising that his gallery should have negotiated with the owners of the works right at the start and have been more involved in the sales. Indeed, Øberg-Pedersen lamented in his letter, the Louisiana Museum should have been more 'sales-minded'.[25]

As in the Louisiana Museum, a 'sales mentality' was not one of the many skills and merits that curators and organisers of Kassel had in their armoury. But there was one exception to this generalisation: the remarkably talented Cologne gallery owner Hein Stünke, who in 1959 had joined the curatorial team, bringing with him his extraordinary ability to gauge the art market, understand its evolution and detect business opportunities. Hein Stünke's impact on documenta, via the activities of the documenta foundation that was set up to produce and sell prints and multiples from Kassel, was felt straight away and would prove both productive and controversial in the years that followed.

Opportunities worth seizing: the Galerie Der Spiegel

[1] Many of them had been on close terms with the former Nacional Socialist rulers. See Mirl Riedmann, 'Das Flüstern der Fussnoten'. In *documenta Studies,* no. 09, June 2020. [https://documenta-studien.de/media/1/documenta_studien_9_Mirl_Redmann.pdf, retrieved in January 2022]

Albeit with some ups and downs, between 1955 and 1968 the team in charge of programming and executing the first editions of documenta remained fairly consistent in certain respects. To begin with, all its members were men, many of them were directly or indirectly part of Arnold Bode's extensive network of personal and professional contacts, and all of them came from the middle and upper classes and were well educated with already well-established and respected careers in the art world: they were historians, critics, curators of museum collections, exhibition curators, university professors, architects and, in some cases, artists.[1]

Only one of them constituted an exception, since he was from a modest family, had no formal academic training and worked not *in* but rather *for* institutions as a service provider. This man was Hein Stünke, founder and owner of Galerie Der Spiegel together with his wife, Eva Stünke. Without a doubt, Stünke was the one who most resolutely brought to the organisation of the first documentas the 'commercial mentality' necessary to promote the fundraising experiment, which would lead to the creation of documenta's own publishing 'label', an entity devoted to the production of artists' prints and editions baptised with a name that honoured the project's lofty ambition: the *documenta foundation*.

Stünke was also the one who most frequently incurred blatant conflicts of interest over the years, no doubt because of his ambiguous position as a disinterested collaborator on the one hand and a provider of professional services on the other, and also because of the aura of power that collaboration with documenta brought to his relationships with artists.

Discreet, mild-mannered and not a fan of the limelight, contrary to the group of men associated with the genesis and success of the initiative, Hein Stünke has to this day remained a somewhat secondary figure in documenta historiography. Yet it is worth pausing to look at his life story, which has not yet been recounted in detail.

Heinrich – 'Hein' – Stünke was born on October 25, 1913, near the city of Oberhausen in the state of Rhineland-Westphalia. He was the only child of a humble family, and his early education consisted of learning the trade of his father, who was a blacksmith. In 1930, at the age of 17, he joined the Hitler Youth, an organisation that indoctrinated young people in National Socialist ideology and gave them basic military training while providing them with some academic or vocational training. Hein Stünke worked as a volunteer with the organisation until 1934, when he became a full-time paid employee. Then, having reached the rank of *Unterbannführer*, he was put in charge of the Training Department of 'Area 8', i.e. Lower Saxony.

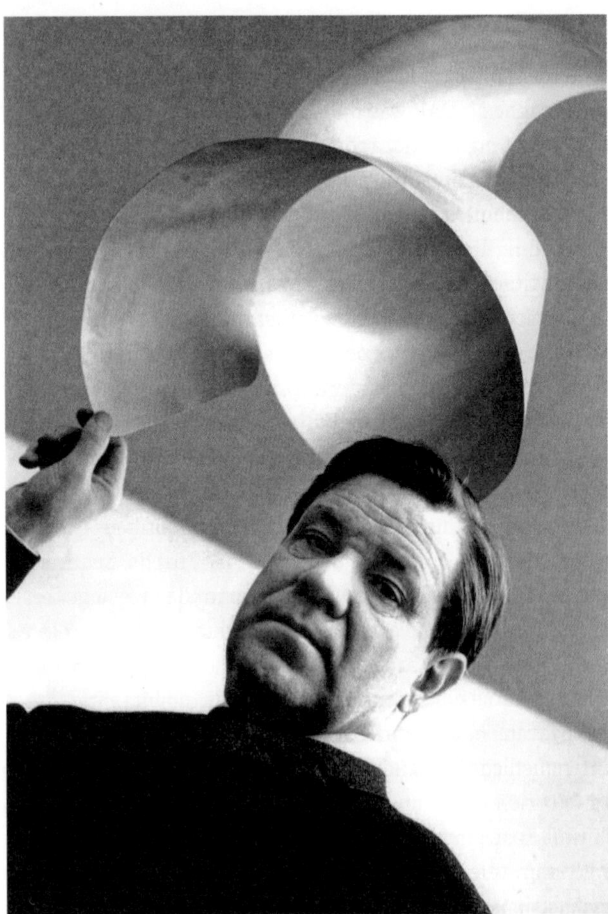

Hein Stünke under Man Ray's *Lampshade*, a
multiple from Edition MAT Collection 64, ca. 1964.
Photo: Rudolf Lichtsteiner / Photostiftung Schweiz.

[2] After Hitler's election victory in 1933, the
NSDAP was flooded with new membership
applications and as a result the party
started admitting only certain candidates,
preferably those with higher education.

[3] Hein Stünke (ed.), *Kampf und Glaube: Gedichte
österreichischer Dichter, 1933-1938*. Potsdam:
Ludwig Voggenreiter Verlag, 1938, p. 87.

[4] Ibíd., p. 88.

[5] The most famous of these was *Es zittern
die morschen Knochen*, whose lines 'Today

Germany belongs to us / tomorrow the whole
world will' were later used in the song *Tomorrow
Belongs to Me* from the musical film *Cabaret*.

[6] Among other positions, from 1967 to 1970
Franz Tumler was also head of Literature
at the West Berlin Academy of the Arts.

[7] In 1939 he was appointed director of the
Mozarteum's popular music school for
young people, and in 1943 he took over
the direction of the Mozart Spielschar.

In 1936, Stünke joined the National Socialist German Workers' Party (NSDAP), whose membership card lists his first profession as 'blacksmith'. By then, admission into the NSDAP was not as easy as it had been before 1933, but Stünke's lack of higher education (which in those days was, along with the mandatory Aryan certificate and an unblemished service record, a key membership requirement) was probably compensated for his years of service in the Hitler Youth.[2] Records of his activity during these years show that it was around this time that he began to become involved in cultural initiatives, taking a particular interest in literature rather than art. In 1938, he published an anthology of Austrian poetry with exalted National Socialist overtones: *Kampf und Glaube: Gedichte österreichischer Dichter, 1933-1938.*[3] In the epilogue to this anthology, which included material by the writer and personal friend Franz Tumler, Stünke explained, *'Kampf und Glaube* brings together the confessions of Austrian poets from the period of struggle of 1933 to 1938. [...] In their own way, they did what many anonymous people of the uprising did, and through their words and ultimately their deeds, became custodians of Germanness in circumstances of maximum danger. A general wish will be fulfilled if the testimonies of that time are made accessible to all the people.'[4] It was at this time that Stünke forged friendships with other men involved in National Socialist cultural organisations, maintaining these relationships after the war.[5] In addition to Tumler, who in the 1940s showed earnest National Socialist leanings and went on to hold important positions in post-war Berlin, his friends included the writer and poet Hans Baumann, lyricist to a large number of songs,[6] member of the National Socialist civil service and, after the war, celebrated author of children's literature; and Cesar Bresgen, an Austrian composer and organist and member of the Hitler Youth, who held various teaching posts during the National Socialist era[7] and later became a respected composer.

In 1939, Hein Stünke was promoted to the rank of *Oberbannführer* and became deputy director of the Cultural Office of the Reich Youth Directorate, the highest level of the Hitler Youth, which was then headed by Baldur von Schirarch. His promotion, however, was short-lived: according to archives he was made redundant. Stünke began to study Philosophy and Art History at university in Berlin but there too, his plans were soon truncated when the outbreak of war saw him conscripted and sent to the front. In 1941, he was seriously wounded and confined to hospital for a brief period, during which time he resumed his studies. He was forced to abandon his studies for a second time when he was called to the front again, where, the following year, on the outskirts of Stalingrad, he sustained renewed, serious injury. After another spell in a military hospital and a stint with the Replacement

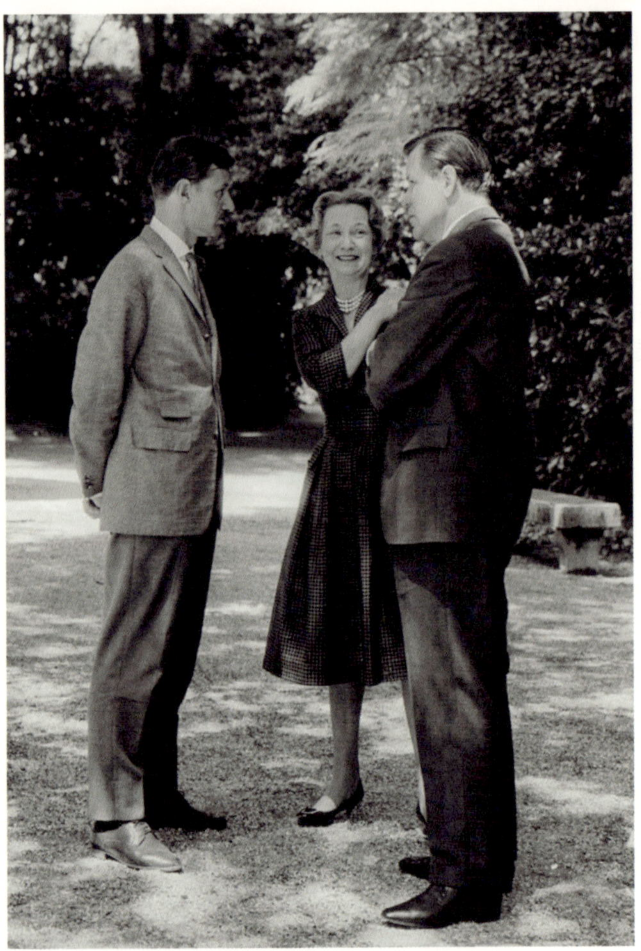

Hein and Eva Stünke in the Danish Pavilion of the Venice
Biennale, 1960, in conversation with an unknown person.
Photo: Galerie Der Spiegel.

[8] Resolution addressed to the Reich Treasurer
of the Hitler Jugend, relative to the request
for funds by way of compensation for services
rendered by Hein Stünke in the Hitler Jugend,
22 September 1942, Federal Archives of
Germany, Koblenz (BArch R 9361-II/ 998878).

[9] Jürgen Schultz, *Die Akademie für Jugendführung
der Hitlerjugend in Braunschweig*,
Braunschweiger Werkstücke, Reihe A, vol. 15.
Braunschweig: Stadtarchiv und Stadtbibliothek
and Weisenhaus Buchdruckerei, 1978, p. 216.

[10] Eva Kahl, *Dürer-Nachfolge in der Reliefplastik
unter besonderer Berücksichtigung des
Eichstätter Meisters Loy Hering*. Doctoral
dissertation, Universität Erlangen, 1940.

[11] Hein Stünke, 'Die Akademie für Jugendführung'.
In *Westermanns Monatshefte*, July 1944, p. 434.

[12] Ibid., p. 431.

Army, he was able to return to Germany, where in mid-1942, on the initiative of the National Socialist politician Kurt Badäus, he submitted a request to the Party Fund for financial aid to see him through to the end of his studies, as had been promised to him on his dismissal before the war. The request was refused due to lack of funds[8] but, thanks to the intercession of Badäus, who at the time was head of the Academy for Youth Leadership of the Hitler Youth in Braunschweig, Stünke was appointed director of one of the courses, an occupation that, given the circumstances, was considered more than suitable for a war casualty.[9]

In 1942, shortly before joining the Academy, Stünke had married Eva Kahl, a cultured woman of his same age born near Cologne into a wealthy family, who shared an interest in art and owned a small collection of antique pieces. Eva held a doctorate in Art History with a thesis on Dürer's influence on relief sculpture[10] and was fluent in French and English. Although she always remained a secondary figure with respect to her husband, as was common in those times, Eva's knowledge and skills as a gallery owner would prove key to the success of the professional ventures they pursued together in the following decades.

From 1942 to 1945, the Stünkes lived in Braunschweig, where Hein had been appointed deputy director of the Hitler Youth's Academy for Youth Leadership. The Academy, an imposing complex of Fascist-style buildings completed only weeks before the outbreak of the war, was the highest-ranking and most prestigious of the schools erected to train the new leaders of the Hitler Youth. 'Of all the Hitler Youth buildings,' Stünke wrote in an article published in 1944, 'the Academy for Youth Leadership ranks first not only in terms of its physical size. It is the highest school of the Hitler Youth and represents the will to form and educate the young political leader corps.'[11] Stünke went on, underlining that candidates to the Academy were not selected on the basis of social class but intellectual ability. The emphasis on personal performance 'calls on the best to prove themselves, regardless of social background. But the selectors also know they must beware the idea of "promoting the poor" that sometimes occurs. National Socialist selection does not mean placing responsibility on those who have not been able to bear it. It is socialist because it places men from the simplest background in a position of leadership if they have the talent for it'.[12] Given his own life story, one can assume he must have strongly identified with such principles.

Hein Stünke remained at the Academy for Youth Leadership until the end of the war. When the Allied troops reached the doors of Braunschweig in late March and early April 1945, he was very nearly drawn back into the conflict when, as highest-ranking staff member of the academy, it fell upon him to lead a meagre 'Stünke Battalion' of about forty soldiers made up of teachers and pupils.[13] Little could be done, however, to defend the position militarily. When the American troops entered Braunschweig on April 11, 1945, the only thing they found was an imposing complex of empty buildings.[14] Along with many others, Hein and Eva Stünke had already fled the city.

The Stünkes made their way on foot across the British occupation zone to Cologne, where they established their home and embarked on a radically different phase in their lives, in which there would be no room to remember or even mention what they had experienced before 1945. Those who knew and dealt with Hein Stünke from 1950 onwards, when he was already a well-known gallery owner in West Germany, agree that he was stubbornly tight-lipped about his National Socialist period. Very little is known about how his attitude must have evolved in relation to his role and political affinities of the 1930s and 1940s.[15] Apart from the few texts he published before the war – all of them of an official nature – barely a trace of his personal impressions of the war comes through from correspondence with friends from his National Socialist period, rare instances of which are kept in the archives. These letters reveal that Stünke was initially confident of the successes the future held for his country, for 'The war has confirmed that the German world has changed: now it can also put the continent in order';[16] even though armed confrontation was not an easy path: war 'is a hard job, I am learning this now. Sometimes I have cursed it – its cruelties are not scarce – those who do not see the whole picture become mired in a thousand problems'.[17] After Germany's defeat, however, his evocation of the

---

[13] Hans Holzträger, *Kampfeinsatz der Hitler Jugend im Chaos der letzten Kriegsmonate.* Dinklage: AGK Verlag, 1995, pp. 46-47.

[14] Sven Keller, *Volksgemeinschaft am Ende: Gesellschaft und Gewalt 1944-1945.* Quellen und Darstellungen zur Zeitgeschichte, vol. 97. Munich: De Gruyter, 2013.

[15] In time he became only slightly more explicit about his political ideas. For example, in the obituary he wrote for Arnold Bode, he referred to Lessing, Hegel and Marx as 'the great blind men of our history'. See Hein Stünke, 'Arnold Bode', op. cit., p. 269.

[16] Hein Stünke, letter to Franz Tumler, July 20, 1940, sent from Przasnysz in central Poland. Deutsches Literaturarchiv Marbach, A: Tumler, Franz D – 92.4.891.

[17] Ibid.

[18] Hein Stünke, letter to Franz Tumler, July 27, 1947. Deutsches Literaturarchiv Marbach, A: Tumler, Franz D – 92.4.891.

[19] Ibid.

[20] Eva Stünke, 'Kann man da ge-hen?' In Klaus Honnef and Hans M. Schmidt (eds.), *Aus den Trümmern: Kunst und Kultur im Rheinland und Westfalen 1945-1952.* Cologne: Rheinland-Verlag, 1985, p. 317.

[21] Ibid.

immediate past became markedly detached. In 1947, he dispatched his life events of the preceding years with a terse summary almost devoid of emotion: '...Joined the infantry, came to the Western Front and took part in the fighting in France. Recovery in Poland, then in Romania, Bulgaria, Lithuania and back to Pruth. Wounded twice, and a third time at Stalingrad. The gods took pity on me and allowed me to recover in Vienna – a wonderful time, that was! Soldier again and then the end, slipping away from the Russians. Somewhere in the centre of Germany I met my wife. Then we walked home, here on the Rhine. We built a house and a shop and set up one of the beautiful western galleries, with a lot of effort (and physical labour). Now we are in the process of setting up a small vintage furniture workshop. That's the plan for the new year. You should come and see what we are doing. And keep your fingers crossed that our wishes come true...'[18]

The 'beautiful western gallery' was none other than the nascent Galerie Der Spiegel, which Hein and Eva had opened in December 1945 in a house in the Deutz district of Cologne that the bombing had spared. 'I want you to know too that not only have we not frozen our vital spirit, but that we want to take part in events and are looking for opportunities that are worth getting involved in...'[19] This is how Hein would describe his outlook after the war ended, an outlook Eva echoed in her own recollections, in which she romanticised the irrepressible will to prosper shared by 'all' – all those, that is, who had survived, who had not been killed or forced to leave the country. There would never be a place in either her or her husband's memories for any of the others. 'And then the miracle: in this impassable desert, people came together to do something. The field of art wouldn't have been different to any other field. Everyone wanted to do something, even if they hardly had anything left, were poorly fed and clothed, with no real home, no future. The scale of the devastation was so enormous it was like a challenge; it gave us courage.'[20] As she later recalled, the gallery got off to a promising start: the first customers were two inspectors who came to check that the business permits were in order, and each bought a watercolour.[21]

Initially, Galerie Der Spiegel began with a small collection of classical art inherited from Eva's parents, but gradually the Stünkes' interest shifted to contemporary art, and increasingly to European artists who had emigrated because of the war, many of whom had been branded 'degenerate' by the Nazis. The Stünkes' close friendship with Max Ernst, whose first retrospective in post-war Germany they organised, opened the door to contacts with this generation. Then there was the Stünkes' interest in French art and culture from before the war, which they developed from 1949-1950 thanks to the professional relationships they nurtured on their

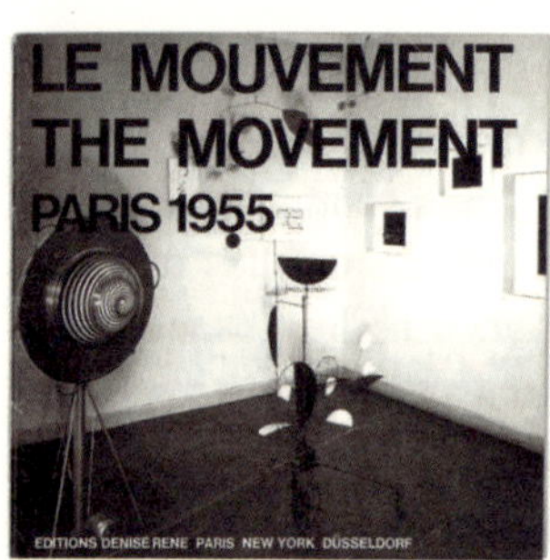

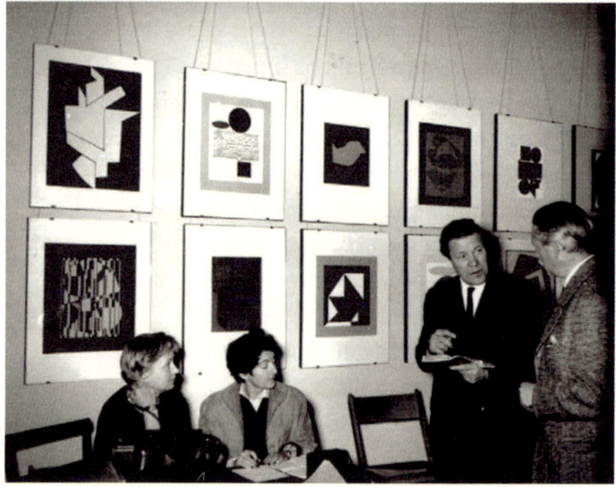

It was in the exhibition catalogue *Le Mouvement / The Movement* [Editions Denis Rene, Paris, 1955] where Victor Vasarely published for the first time his text 'The Movement: Notes for a Manifesto', also known as 'Yellow Manifesto', where he advocated the multiplication and seriality of artworks. Below, Eva Stünke, Denis Rene, Hein Stünke and Richard Mortensen in the Galerie Der Spiegel during an exhibition with works by Victor Vasarely, 1959.
Photo: Galerie Der Spiegel.

[22] Ibid.

[23] Aimé Maeght trained as a lithographer.

[24] The first graphic portfolio published by Galerie Der Spiegel was a series of twelve lithographs by the German painter Friedrich Vordemberge, published in 1949 and put on sale for DM 85.

regular trips to the French capital. As a result, Galerie Der Spiegel became
the first to showcase the School of Paris in Germany in the 1950s: Matisse
with his book *Jazz*, the graphic work of Picasso, the sculptures of Henri
Laurens, the painting of Ferdinand Léger, André Masson… The gallery's
catalogue would soon incorporate other European artists well known
in France, among them Joan Miró, Marino Marini and Victor Vasarely,
whose first exhibitions in Germany were put on by the Stünkes; and little
by little, thanks to the contacts obtained through documenta, it would
expand further with a good number of American exponents of Abstract
Expressionism and Pop art.

In 1948 Galerie Der Spiegel moved to Richartzstrasse 10 in the centre
of Cologne, where the Stünkes began to exhibit more contemporary works,
sometimes provoking angry reactions from passers-by as Eva recalled.[22]
Not long afterwards, the gallery established a publishing company of the
same name at the initiative of the writer and translator Albrecht Fabri, a
bibliophile and close collaborator of the Stünkes who was well connected
to the local art scene. Fabri's drive, coupled with the influential example
set by the French gallery owners Aimé and Marguerite Maeght, who had
also started publishing graphic artwork from their gallery,[23] encouraged the
Stünkes to explore this territory, first with lithographs[24] and later with silk
screen prints, an old technique adopted by the painter Fritz Winter, who
had learned to use it at the Bauhaus. In 1950, Galerie Der Spiegel published
its first portfolio of prints – by Franz Winter – using this silkscreen, which
Vasarely would later employ constantly.

Convinced that graphic art would be a good commercial niche, in the
mid-1950s the Stünkes decided to set up their own printing and bookbinding
workshop too. This workshop would soon expand to include framing
and the manufacture of simple furniture, first in a studio in Cologne's
Trajanstrasse and later in a building in the tiny village of Schüller (Eifel),
some 100 km southwest of Cologne, where the Stünkes had begun to go for
occasional moments of relaxation. This workshop, which at one point had as
many as fifty employees, supported the gallery financially in its early stages
and ensured its survival. Over the years, the modern framing services offered
by Galerie Der Spiegel would be requested by the Kestner Gesellschaft in
Hanover, the Städel Museum in Frankfurt, and other German museums and
galleries, as well as by institutions such as the German Academic Exchange
Service (DAAD), the Goethe Institute, and documenta itself, for which the
Stünkes soon became regular suppliers.

In addition to the Maeghts, with whom the Stünkes had a professional
relationship, and the couple Otto and Etta Stangl, who had opened their

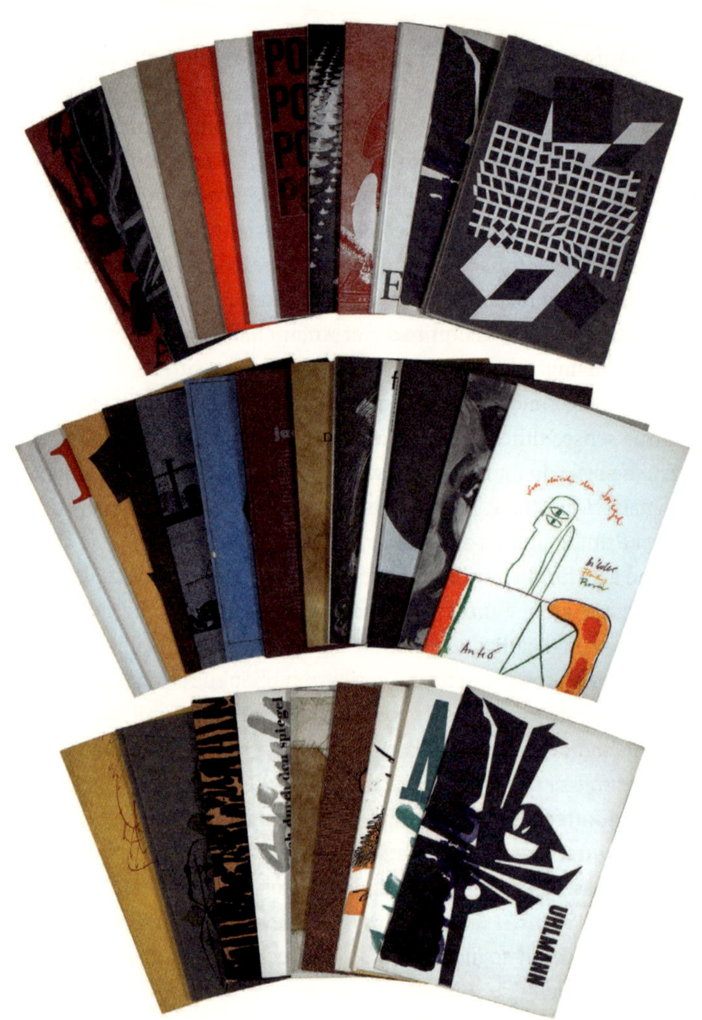

Geh durch den Spiegel (complete series).
Cologne: Galerie Der Spiegel, 1954-1966.
Photo: Galerie Der Spiegel.

[25] Martin Schieder, *Im Blick des anderen: Die deutsch-französischen Kunstbeziehungen 1945-1959*. Freiburg: De Gruyter, 2005, p. 198.

[26] Years later, Hein Stünke would describe the Cassirers as 'emancipated Jews, educated in the German spirit'. Hein Stünke, 'Das Geschäft mit der Kunst'. In Klaus Honnef and Hans M. Schmidt (eds.), op. cit., p. 440.

[27] *Der Querschnitt - Das Magazin der aktuellen Ewigkeitswerte*, published between 1924 and 1933.

[28] See Regina Schmidt, 'Die Galerie Der Spiegel und der Bundesdeutsche Markt'. In *Sediment*, no. 1. Bonn: Zentralarchiv für Deutsche und Internationale Kunstmarktforschung – ZADIK, 1994, pp. 21-24.

gallery in Munich in 1947 to focus on avant-garde art and the rehabilitation of the work of 'degenerate artists',[25] other significant references in the trajectory of Galerie Der Spiegel were two dealers from the previous generation, both of them sons of the wealthy Jewish bourgeoisie:[26] Paul Cassirer, who introduced the Impressionists to Germany in the first decades of the twentieth century, and Alfred Flechtheim, editor of the pompously titled magazine *The Cross-Section: The Magazine of Contemporary Eternal Values*,[27] which had focused on the cultural scene of the 1920s and 1930s. With their work, both Cassirer and Flechtheim had drawn attention to the possibility of using publishing as a nexus to connect with the higher echelons of the enlightened middle class, something that the Stünkes seized upon.[28] But, in this sense, although no documentary basis has been found to prove it, there can be little doubt that the Maeght gallery's most famous publication, the magazine *Derrière le miroir* ['Behind the Mirror'] must have been a major influence. Printed uninterruptedly from 1946 to 1982, *Derrière le miroir* functioned as a forum for discussion, a source of information and a way of distributing the graphic work of the artists represented by the gallery. Echoes of the Maeght publication resonate strongly in one of the Stünkes' most important publishing projects: the series of bibliophile periodicals *Geh durch den Spiegel* ['Go Through the Mirror'], whose first issue, dedicated to Marino Marini, was published in 1954.

Geh durch den Spiegel* ran until 1966, with a total of 48 issues released in limited editions of between 100 and 400 copies. Each issue included original graphic work and literary texts and was almost always dedicated to a single artist (with two exceptions, a collaborative issue between Jean Arp and Max Ernst, and one devoted to English prints), and they served both as *livres d'artiste* – direct descendants of the French tradition of the *livres de peintre* – and as monographs of a very particular style. Over the years, issues were dedicated to numerous European avant-garde painters – Max Ernst, Hans Arp, Wols, Karel Appel, Ben Nicholson, HAP Grieshaber, Marino Marini, Victor Vasarély, Horst Antes, Dorothea Tanning, Karl Gerstner, Serge Poliakoff, Ernst Wilhelm Nay and François Morellet – but also to artists from other movements such as Dada, Surrealism, Op art, COBRA and Informalism.

The *Geh durch den Spiegel* series would not be the only publishing project the Stünkes carried out. Besides the *Spiegelschriften* collection, which included the books *Paramythen* by Max Ernst (1955/1970) and *Gespräche mit Marcel Duchamp* by Pierre Cabanne (1972), the gallery's publishing house also reprinted bibliophile works, among them Max Ernst's *Histoire Naturelle II*, first published in 1926.

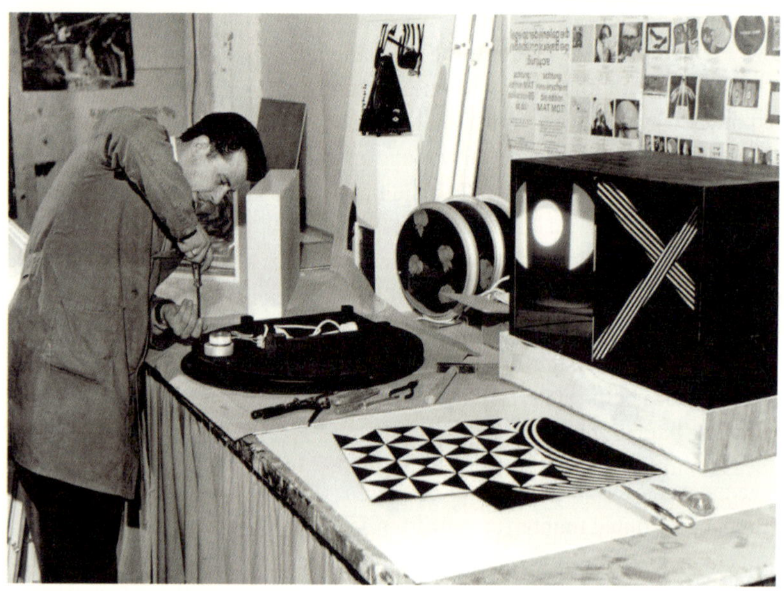

Workshop of Galerie Der Spiegel during the
production of multiples of the MAT Edition, 1967.
Photo: Dr. Salchow / Galerie Der Spiegel.

²⁹ Karl Gerstner and Daniel Spoerri (eds.),
*Kunstwerke, die bewegen, die sich bewegen
oder bewegen lassen. Multiplizierte
demokratische Kunst und Originale in
Serien aus den 60n Jahren.* Cologne:
Galerie Der Spiegel, 1993, p. 3.

³⁰ For a detailed history of Edition MAT see
Katherina Vatsella, op. cit., 1998.

³¹ Daniel Spoerri (ed.), *Material. Zeitschrift
für konkrete Dichtung und bildende
Kunst,* which Spoerri published four
issues of between 1958 and 1960.

³² Daniel Spoerri, letter to Josef
Albers, September 1959. Quoted in
Katherina Vatsella, op. cit., p. 37.

³³ The same stimulus was driving other artists on
both sides of the Atlantic to produce their first
artists' books: Dieter Roth released *Kinderbuch
/ Children's Book* in 1957 and *Buch / Book AA*
in 1960, while Ed Ruscha published his first
edition of *Twenty-Six Gasoline Stations* in 1963.

³⁴ As had been the case with the previous editions,
the new 'Collection 65' was exhibited in many
galleries and institutions internationally,
including the Museum of Modern Art in the
spring of 1965. At MoMA, however, interestingly,
it was not shown in the usual exhibition rooms
but in the so-called 'Art Lending Service Gallery',
to which only friends of the museum had
access. During the show, multiples were on
sale for between 90 and 150 dollars. See Karl
Gerstner and Henri Stierlin (eds.), *Der Geist der
Farbe. Karl Gerstner und seine Kunst.* Stuttgart:
Deutsche Verlags-Anstalt (DVA), 1981, p. 19.

The Stünkes' real publishing innovation, however, was not any of these collections, but rather their wholehearted embrace of a new genre whose commercial viability was still a total unknown: the artist's multiple.

Galerie Der Spiegel began working on multiples in 1963 via a collaboration with 'Edition MAT', an initiative launched by Daniel Spoerri in 1959. Stünke would later recall that 'Edition MAT owes its genesis to friendship: Daniel Spoerri's friendship with Karl Gerstner, and Karl Gerstner's with me'.[29] 'MAT' was the acronym for 'Multiplication d'Art Transformable', an idea of Spoerri's that consisted of creating artistic objects in series with neither a fixed nor stable format.[30] In Daniel Spoerri's own words: 'Starting from the idea of the *material* magazine,[31] which didn't set out to inform about anything but to represent the thing itself, to carry it out, I came upon the idea of multiplying objects in an edition, without destroying or altering the content they possess as originals; of making an edition of multiplied original works and not reproductions. [...] The entire edition would have a uniform price, which means that each work would cost $50, regardless of who made it. This is the social standpoint of this edition, which does not aim to convert the value of the individual work into a commercial value.'[32] Inspired by this idea, between 1959 and 1960 Spoerri personally commissioned, produced, publicised and distributed limited editions of works by Marcel Duchamp, Josef Albers, Paul Bury, Bruno Munari, Dieter Roth, Rafael Soto, Jean Tinguely and Victor Vasarely, among others.

Spoerri's ambition was not only to explore ways of involving the viewer in artistic creation – through the movement of the pieces, which would be always changing and allow for a certain amount of viewer interaction – but above all to bypass the official channels of the art market and open up an alternative path to commercialisation in galleries that would, thanks to low prices, enable a more egalitarian access to the artistic object.[33] By the end of 1960, however, the effort involved in being in sole charge of all the phases of production had left Spoerri exhausted and, despite the project's growing popularity, he decided to throw it all in. But in 1963 the Swiss artist and graphic designer Karl Gerstner, captivated by the idea, persuaded him to give it another try, together, and this time under the tagline 'Originals in Series'. Arman, Raymond Hains, Arnulf Reiner, Man Ray and Niki de Saint Phalle were some of the artists who joined the MAT Edition at this second stage, for which Spoerri and Gerstner drew up a contract with Galerie Der Spiegel, requiring the Stünke workshop to produce the multiples and the gallery to market them.[34]

Certainly, the relationship with the gallery crushed the democratising spirit of the initiative, but in exchange it relieved the artists of work and the

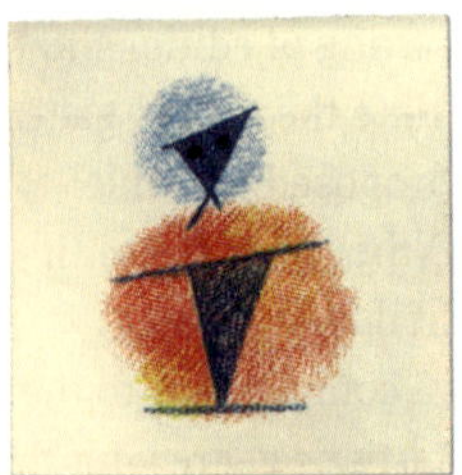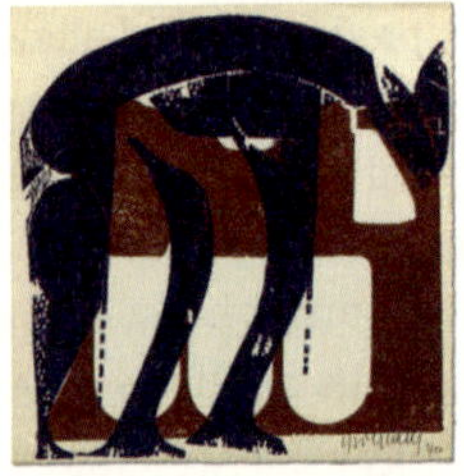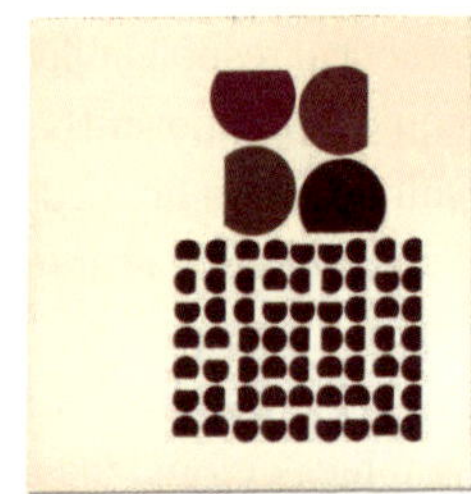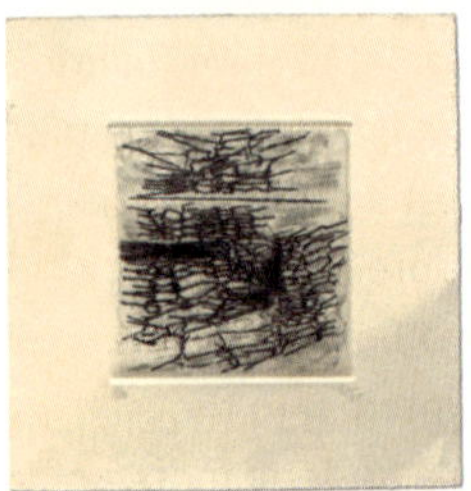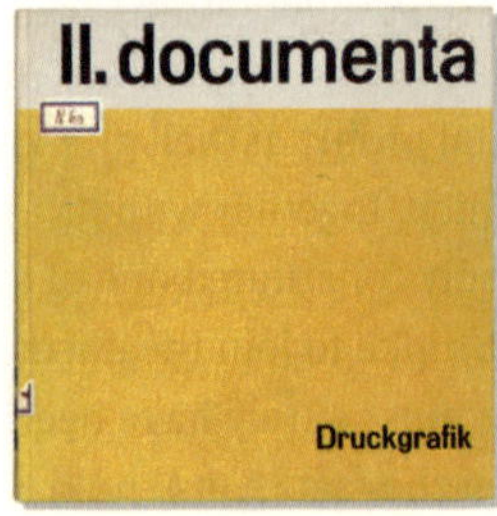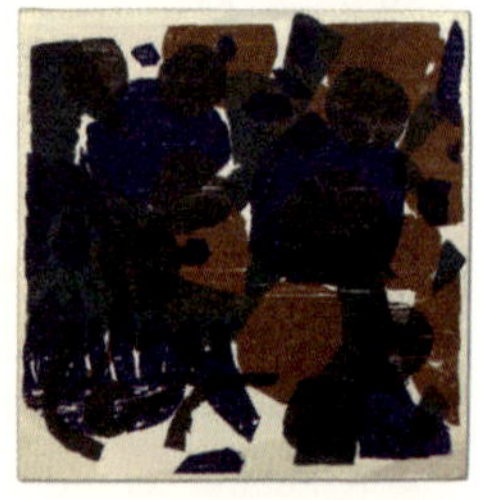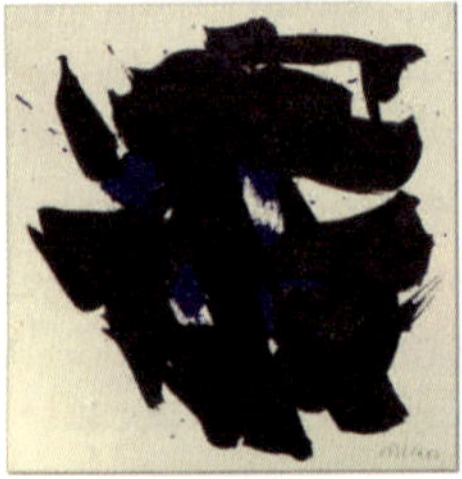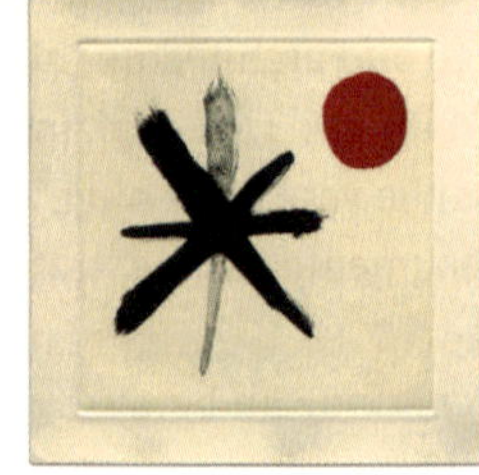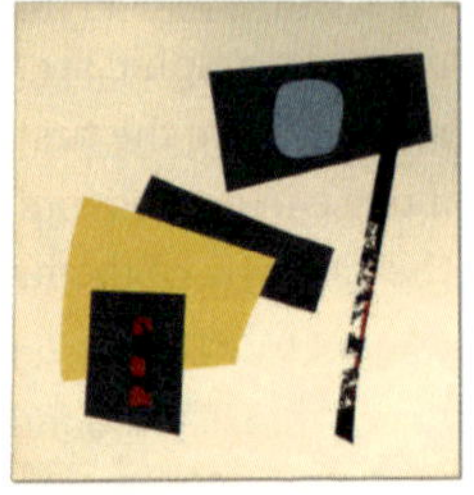

Catalogue of the print exhibition at documenta II: limited edition (300 ex.) with an accompanying series of prints. Clockwise, works by Max Ernst, HAP Grieshaber, Viktor Vasarely, Hann Trier, Pierre Soulages, Joan Miró, Berto Lardera and Ernst Wilhelm Nay. Kassel: documenta, 1959. Photo: documenta archiv.

[35] Music, dance, film and theatre had also been included in the initial plans for documenta but had had to be almost completely scrapped as they were too ambitious for the resources available.

[36] Long before documenta 6 (1977), usually noted for being the first and only time the programme devoted an exhibition to the genre of artists' books.

[37] Erhart Kårstner was director of this library from 1950 to 1968 and is credited with building up an important collection of contemporary bibliophilia. In the summer of 1968, coinciding with documenta IV, Kårstner curated the exhibition *Maler machen Bücher* ['Painters make books'] at the Kunstverein in Kassel.

[38] Erich Pfeiffer-Belli, "Industrieform und Plakat. Eine Ausstellung anlässlich der Kasseler documenta III'. In *Süddeutsche Zeitung*, August 28, 1964, documenta archiv, AA, d03, 10.

[39] *Grafik und Objekte: vervielfältigte Kunst*, documenta IV, Kassel, 1968. Among the books by Dieter Roth exhibited in this show was *Buch / Book AC*, 1964, a cardboard box containing 24 unbound sheets of paper, visible through several openings in the box's lid, and based on the same principle of variability as the book *Buch AA23*, 1958-1959, which had been Roth's contribution to the MAT Edition.

practical responsibilities of production and allowed a string of editions to come to light over the next two years. However, with time the artists-gallery collaboration broke down, and in 1965 Hein Stünke proposed to Daniel Spoerri that he acquire for the token sum of DM 2000 the rights to continue using the name 'Edition MAT' under his sole responsibility.

For Galerie Der Spiegel, the multiples served as a complement to the graphic editions; the fact that they represented a new artistic genre with the enormous possibilities for experimentation that Spoerri, Kerstner and other artists believed it to be, was secondary. Even so, Edition MAT gave Galerie Der Spiegel an experimental profile as well as a knowledge of the potential of this market segment which, together with its interest and contacts in avant-garde art, undoubtedly constituted one of the more compelling reasons for inviting Hein Stünke to join the documenta Board in 1959.

Stünke's knowledge must surely have been of interest to the organisers of Kassel, given the fact that Arnold Bode's understanding of art as an expanded field, where not only painting and sculpture but also drawing, graphic art, design and architecture all belong, had prevailed already since the first exhibition.[35] This explains why graphic art had had a place in documenta from the very beginning, as the display of prints in the cafeteria of the first documenta demonstrates, with pieces by Picasso among others.

This interest would continue and grow over time. Precisely because of the interconnectedness of prints, artists' editions and, by extension, artists' publications, it was in the graphic art section of documenta where artists' books first made a timid appearance.[36] The exhibition of graphic art organised for documenta II was complemented by a section of 'illustrated' books, curated by Erhart Kästner, then director of the Herzog August Bibliothek in Wolfenbütel.[37] And a limited edition of 300 copies of the documenta II catalogue dedicated to this exhibition was brought out, which included inserts with prints by artists, and of these, a 'luxury' edition of 20 exemplars was made in which the prints were given larger margins and were numbered and signed. At documenta III, certain artists' publications – in this case posters – also featured in the applied arts exhibition on view at the Kassel Municipal School of Arts and Crafts, which brought together industrial design pieces, photographs, elements of typography and calligraphy as well as the said posters, which were particularly well received by the press.[38]

Finally, in documenta IV, the exhibition *Graphic Work and Objects: Serial Art*[39] also included books – not as much contemporary bibliophilia as in 1959, but rather pieces by some of the artists considered as 'founders'

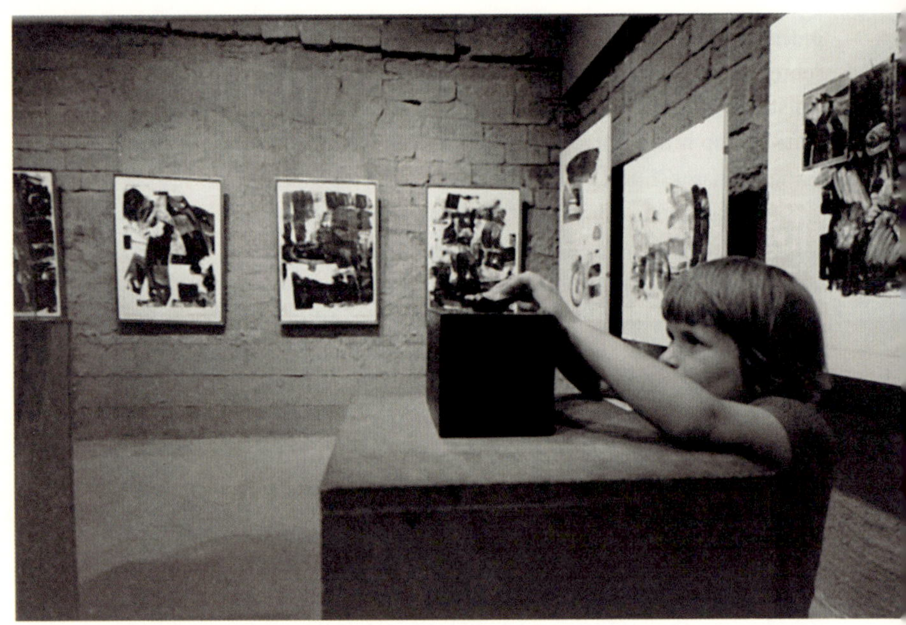

View of the exhibition *Grafik und Objekte: Vervielfältigte Kunst*
[Prints and Objects: Multiplied Art], documenta IV, 1968.
Photo: Werner Kohn / documenta archiv.

40 Birgit Maria Sturm, 'Diese diffizile Ware Kunst.
Ein Interview mit dem Kölner Galeristen Hein
Stünke über die Entstehungsgeschichte
des Kölner Kunstmarktes'. In *Art
Position*, 5, no. 22, 1993, p. 21.

41 Kristian Handberg, op. cit.

of the artist's book genre. Among them, notably Dieter Roth, who was represented with items from the personal collection of Dietrich Helms, artist and professor at the Hamburg School of Fine Arts and member of the working committee for the graphic work shown in Kassel.

***

But let us return to the months prior to 1959, when Bode and Haftmann, together with their minuscule team, were hard at work with preparations for the second edition of documenta, a sequel that had not been envisaged initially but which in view of the public and critical success of the 1955 documenta was eagerly anticipated and defended. With a distinctly precarious working structure and so little time to organise such an enormously ambitious project, Hein Stünke's knowledge and contacts were undeniably instrumental in obtaining the works desired – particularly those destined for the graphic art section – and resolving numerous technical aspects of the production, such as the framing of the pieces. Contrary to the services Stünke offered documenta as a provider, his collaboration with the curatorial team was to be unpaid. Arnold Bode and the other organisers must have therefore thought it perfectly natural to entrust Hein and Eva – the only gallery owners on the team – with the task of managing a small space for the sale of prints for the duration of the exhibition, a space improvised at the last minute and strategically located next to the graphic art section. 'The real actors of the documenta – Haftmann, Bode, Zwirner and von Buttlar – received a fee for their work, but I didn't. Arnold Bode was embarrassed by this, but there simply wasn't any more money in the documenta coffers. So one day he said to me, "Here's what we'll do: you're going to get a stand, three metres by two, and you can sell your prints there." It was more a consolation than a fee. But then the unforeseeable happened: the graphics stand was a huge success. It was an unexpected surprise for me, too.'[40]

The decision to sell prints at documenta II – which was again a success with a turnout of over 130,000 people, was well grounded, for several reasons. Firstly, it helped turn the exhibition tour into a 'popular experience, where modern art could be enjoyed in a spectacular setting accompanied by contemporary design interiors, cafés, bars and other facilities'.[41] The significant amount of money the sales made also helped to balance documenta's accounts and brought some financial stability to Stünke's gallery, which was being kept afloat largely by the printmaking and bookbinding workshop and framing services. Thirdly, as the prices

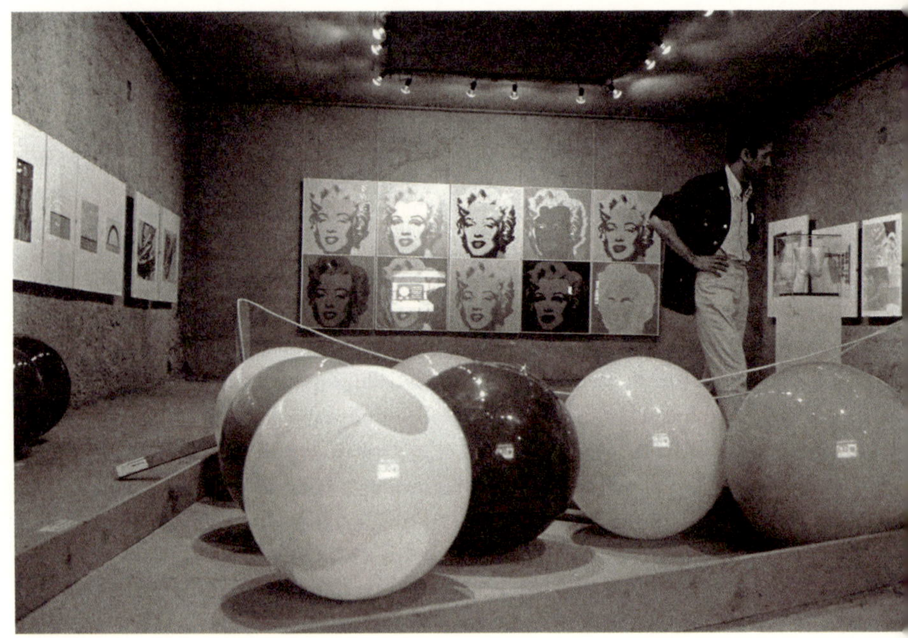

View of the exhibition *Grafik und Objekte: Vervielfältigte Kunst*
[Prints and Objects: Multiplied Art], documenta IV, 1968.
Photo: Werner Kohn / documenta archiv.

---

42 Katharina Schmidt, 'Geh durch den
Spiegel. Laudatio anlässlich der Verleihung
des Art Cologne-Preses 1991 an Hein
Stünke'. In *Sediment*, no. 1. Bonn: Zentral
Archiv für Deutsche und Internationale
Kunstmarktforschung, 1994, pp. 15-20.

of the prints were more affordable than those of the original works, the inclusion of a sales stand for graphic work represented a stance taken in favour of the democratisation of the access to art. In spite of, or perhaps, because of this, the older generation of art dealers saw it as a profanation of the intimate relationship between art work and collector. But the fact is, Stünke's stand effected change on a deeper level, which had to do with how art was displayed, with the consumption habits of a society undergoing a profound transformation and with the perception of the exclusivity of art as a marker of class – aspects that were now being reordered into a new set of relationships, different from those that had prevailed before the war. 'Hein Stünke had offered himself for the task in Kassel, and the small stand in Bellevue he had been given to compensate the cost turned out to be a success. Because people bought. A tremendous frenzy for graphic work was unleashed. Rudolf Zwirner, who as documenta secretary remembers the situation very well, speaks of a "breakthrough in general awareness". Suddenly people understood that for eighty or a hundred marks, those pieces could be yours to buy, that you could become a collector.'[42]

documenta foundation's multiples and editions

[1] Hein Stünke, 'Arnold Bode', op. cit., p. 268.

[2] Lemke quoted in Harald Kimpel, op. cit., p. 106.

[3] Minutes of the meeting of the documenta GmbH, January 17, 1961, documenta archiv, AA, d03, 72, fol. 4–15.

[4] Whose full name in German was 'documenta Gesellschaft GmbH'. 'GmbH' is broadly equivalent to 'Ltd'. [Translator's note.]

The runaway success of the sale of graphic work that Hein and Eva Stünke had pulled off in documenta II in 1959 encouraged the organising committee to include the commercialisation of prints and artist's editions in their plans for the upcoming third edition. It quickly became apparent, moreover, that the idea could serve several purposes, including not only fundraising but also the consolidation of the various networks of documenta allies that were willing to lend support free of charge. Arnold Bode was well aware of the enormous relevance that such allies could have and responded to anything that helped to bring them on board with instant enthusiasm. As Hein Stünke would recall after Bode's death in 1977, this attitude was characteristic of Bode: 'The realisation of such an ambitious plan required the help and cooperation of many knowledgeable and well-connected people. The *circle of friends*, as he called it, was very important to him. Through it he gained numerous contacts, insights and information. He was ingenious when it came to making friends. He made the most of his friends' services and sometimes put them under a lot of strain, but he was also untiringly generous and always ready to do whatever he could. It is his merit to have united the very different temperaments that sat on the Board of the first and subsequent documenta exhibitions.'[1]

So it had been already with Club 53, the group of friends that met regularly at Bode's home and in the company of whom Bode had first outlined the basic concepts for the first documenta, which was organised along similar lines. Indeed, Heinz Lemke, president of the Society for Western Art of the Twentieth Century, described Club 53 as 'the embryo of documenta'.[2]

Over time, Bode devised a range of formulae which would crystallise these existing networks into structures of a more or less official nature. His objectives are evident already in the earliest records concerning the preparations of the exhibition: in the first days of 1961, in a summary of the main ideas he planned to present at the next documenta board meeting, Bode included an organisation chart which showed these networks and posed the question: 'How might documenta be carried out?' Underneath was the answer in the form of a list of three organisms: documenta GmbH, the Circle of Friends of documenta and the documenta foundation.[3]

Until then, only documenta GmbH[4] existed as such. It had been established as a limited company in 1959, shortly before documenta II, to replace the original Society for Western Art of the Twentieth Century, and the City of Kassel and the Hessen region were its main stakeholders. They had initially been joined by the painter Fritz Winter with a symbolic capital contribution of DM 600, which would be returned to him some years later when the society was fully institutionalised.

Bode-Plan

Während der Gartenschau 1955 soll in Kassel eine Ausstellung
mit dem Titel "Europäische Kunst des 2o. Jahrhunderts" statt-
finden.

Gründe: Das Beispiel anderer Städte, in denen eine Gartenschau war,
zeigt, daß eine derartige Veranstaltung mit einer Anzahl ein-
ander ablösender kultureller Veranstaltungen verbunden sein
muß, um die Gäste mehrere Tage in Kassel festzuhalten. Wer
Tagungen besucht, die ebenfalls ~~tunlichst~~ in dieser Zeit nach
Kassel gezogen werden, muß auch kulturelle Anziehungspunkte
~~schaffen~~, lebendiges Kulturleben demonstrieren.

Eine Ausstellung europäischer Kunst des 2o. Jahrhunderts hat
es in Deutschland nach dem Krieg noch nicht gegeben. Sie ist
aber notwendig, für die Künstler, um von deutscher Seite den
Kontakt wieder aufzunehmen, für das Land Hessen, um die über-
lokale Bedeutung der Gartenschau zu unterstreichen und außer der
Fachleuten auch die kulturell Interessierten zu erfassen, für
den Bund, weil der Gedanke einer gemeinsamen europäischen Kunst
im Zeichen der Europa-Bewegung förderungswert und -wichtig ist.
Kassel ist die deutsche Stadt, die für eine derartige Ausstellung prädestiniert ~~xxxxxixxxxx~~ ist. Kassel liegt im Zonen-
grenzgebiet, ist sehr zerstört gewesen und sehr aktiv im Auf-
bau. 3o Kilometer von der Zonengrenze entfernt den Europa-Geden-
ken in einer Kunstausstellung zu manifestieren ist eine bei-
spielhafte Tat von symbolhafter Bedeutung. Kassel ist nicht
belastet durch Künstlerbünde und politisch-künstlerische Ver-
flechtungen, die belasten könnten. Kassel will bewußt nicht an
irgend eine alte Tradition anknüpfen, wodurch sofort Parteien
~~xxxxx~~ entstünden. Kassel will mit dieser Ausstellung eine Tradition bilden, denn ihre Grundidee ist ausbaufähig.

Arnold Bode, 'Bode-Plan', typed text, undated [1953].
Source: documenta archiv, AA, d01, 20, fol. 49.

---

[5] Minutes of the meeting of the documenta
GmbH, January 17, 1961, op. cit.

[6] Minutes of the meeting of the documenta
Supervisory Board, January 23, 1962,
documenta archiv, AA, d03, 70, fol. 165-169.

[7] Statutes of the association 'Circle of Friends
of documenta', undated, documenta
archiv, AA, d02, 38, fol. 17-23.

The Circle of Friends and the documenta foundation, on the other hand, were still little more than proposals in 1961. In relation to the former, in his summary Arnold Bode suggested, 'We should constitute a committee to set up the Circle of Friends for the Promotion of documenta. Who could join this three-person preparatory committee? The aim of the committee would be to form a commission like the one in the current programme of the Society for the Promotion of State Theatre. The committee could also address questions concerning the future new museum in Kassel, since this museum is closely related to the idea of documenta. It would serve financial and conceptual purposes in favour of the promotion of the documenta idea.'[5]

Although no documents have been found attesting to the other organisers' reaction to this proposal of Bode's, we can assume it was accepted since it began to materialise a year later: in January 1962, the agenda of the documenta Supervisory Board meeting includes the proposal to invite the President of the District of Kassel, Fritz Hoch, to chair the Circle of Friends of documenta, and Siegfried Hagen, who had already expressed his desire to collaborate, to oversee its finances.[6] In September of that year, the documenta secretariat sent letters to the Mayor and City Council informing them that the preliminary steps for the creation of the documenta Circle of Friends were gathering pace, and a draft of its statutes had been submitted to the City Council for approval. An unsigned and undated copy of this draft is kept in the Archive and reads, 'The association "Circle of Friends of documenta" is constituted with the aim of promoting documenta GmbH and the cultural objectives this society has set itself. Inscription on the register of associations has not taken place. The aim of the association is primarily to promote documenta, to collaborate in the execution of the documenta GmbH's objectives, to raise additional funds for events organised by said documenta GmbH and to place them at its disposal. The association has no intention of deriving a profit, either for itself or for its members.'[7]

As explicitly stated in these statutes, the Circle of Friends of documenta was never registered in the Kassel Register of Associations. It is therefore hard to say when it began functioning or how long it lasted, although most probably it was dissolved in June 1972, when, coinciding with the inauguration of documenta 5, it was replaced by the documenta forum, a registered association that still exists today, whose purpose is to build support among civil society to promote documenta and strengthen its links with Kassel. Strikingly, already in its first statutes, the forum expressed in its mission statement a highly evolved conception that veered away from the initial idea of 'periodic event' to consider documenta a permanent fixture

<u>Abschrift</u>

Kassel'64   7. Mai 1963
DOCUMENTA-RAT   N/Kl
der Vorsitzende

An den Vorsitzenden
des Aufsichtsrates der documenta-G.m.b.H.
Herrn Oberbürgermeister Dr. Karl Branner
<u>Kassel</u>
Rathaus

Sehr geehrter Herr Dr. Branner,

ich darf Sie von dem Beschluß unterrichten, den der documenta-
Rat zum Abschluß seiner Sitzung in der Berliner Akademie der
Künste am 3.5.1963 in Anwesenheit von Herrn Bürgermeister
Karl Hemfler gefaßt hat. Der Beschluß hat folgenden Wortlaut:

> Der documenta-Rat hält die Verwirklichung der documenta III
> im Rahmen des ihm vorliegenden Finanzierungsvoranschlages
> von 1,4 Millionen DM für möglich mit der Einschränkung,
> daß für die bauliche Ausgestaltung außerhalb des Voran-
> schlages ein Betrag von etwa 100.000,- DM erforderlich ist.
> Der documenta-Rat erklärt, daß er um die Aufbringung dieses
> Betrages bemüht sein wird.

Zur Frage der Bereitschaft des documenta-Rates, um die Beschaffung
der fehlenden 100.000,- DM bemüht zu sein, darf ich folgende
Erläuterungen geben:

Herr Professor Dr. Kurt Martin, der Generaldirektor der Bayerischen
Staatsgemäldesammlungen, schlägt vor, 4 oder 5 Bildhauer von euro-
päischem Rang zu bitten, kleinformatige Gußmodelle zum Bronzeguß
in einer Auflage von etwa 100 Exemplaren zur Verfügung zu stellen.
Diese Kleinbronzen könnten dann zu einem Preis von etwa 300,- DM
während der Ausstellung verkauft werden. Die Selbstkosten (ein-
schließlich Steuern u.a.) betragen nach bereits vorhandenen Erfah-
rungen etwa 100,- DM je Stück, so daß mit einem Reinerlös von
200,- DM je Exemplar gerechnet werden kann. Der Verkauf von

- 2 -

Herbert von Buttlar, letter to Karl Brenner [former
Mayor of Kassel], May 7, 1965, where he attributes
the idea of raising funds for the documenta
organisation by selling serial works to Kurt Martin.
Source: documenta archiv, AA, d03, 78a, fol. 145.

[8] Statutes of the documenta Forum,
adopted and signed June 16, 1972,
documenta archiv, AA, d05, 120.

[9] Herbert von Buttlar, untitled text,
undated [1968]. Zentralarchiv
für Deutsche und internationale
Kunstmarktforschung - ZADIK, A1, IV, 004.

[10] Andreas Vowinckel, 'Ist Kunst, was bedeutende
Künstler machen? Fragen zur Geschichte
und Tätigkeit der documenta foundation
1964-1977 sowie zum Selbstverständnis
der documenta'. In Andreas Vowinckel and
Harald Kimpel, *Die documenta foundation.
Ein Modell der Selbstfinanzierung.*
Marburg: Jonas Verlag, 2002, p. 20.

whose remit and impact went beyond the limits of artistic practice: 'The aim of the association is to promote documenta as an institution of Kassel. It views documenta as a permanent cultural and social commitment that extends beyond the narrower confines of art and embraces other cultural and social issues and institutions.'[8] This was an unequivocal sign that, by 1970, the institutional consolidation of documenta, which was heading towards its fifth edition, was a reality and already well advanced.

In his 1961 draft, Bode indicated that the third of the structural pillars he considered necessary for the project was a 'documenta foundation', a tool that would serve to raise funds by channelling the collaboration of another key collective: the community of artists. This, in fact, was something the organising team had been thinking about for some time. Kurt Martin, museum curator and member of the organising team from documenta II to IV, has been credited with the idea of creating a non-profit association dedicated to the production of editions donated by artists: 'During the preparations for documenta III it became clear that, despite the subsidies received from the City of Kassel, the federal government and the State of Hesse, there were still not enough resources to mount the sculpture exhibition in the Orangerie. Kurt Martin then suggested asking the artists to help. The sale of the works they donated would provide the extra funds. This suggestion became a reality with the creation of the documenta foundation (a registered non-profit association). Since then, the foundation is responsible for raising funds to support special areas within the documenta exhibitions.'[9]

Although publicly presented in June 1964, coinciding with the opening of documenta III, the fact is that the 'registered association *documenta foundation*', as it was officially called, did not exist legally until October 27 of that year. The choice of name is rather paradoxical as it does not correspond entirely with the reality of the facts: the new entity was clearly not a foundation in the strict sense, but an association, and furthermore it was not named in German, as Bode had imagined years earlier, but in English. Andreas Vowinckel, who for years served as the foundation's secretary, would later point out that this name, drawing inspiration from American foundations, was intended to 'reflect the international aspirations of the new association and its field of activity'.[10]

This slight mismatch between reality and public image was mirrored in the first statutes explaining the foundation's mission, which made no reference at all to documenta: 'The aim of the association is to promote general interest in the cultural field and to promote the fine arts in particular, by (a) holding exhibitions in which paintings, sculptures,

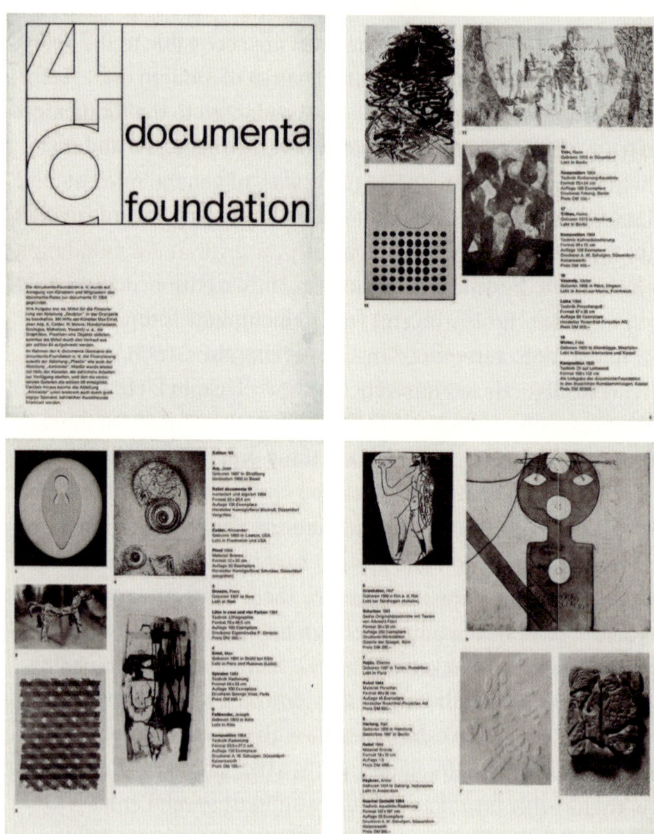

Edition 64 – documenta foundation [brochure], Kassel, 1964.

11 Statutes of the documenta foundation
e. V. (first version), October 27, 1964,
documenta archiv, AA, d04, 31, fol. 46-50.

12 Statutes of the documenta foundation e.
V. (second version), undated, Zentralarchiv
für Deutsche und internationale
Kunstmarktforschung - ZADIK, A1, IV, 004.

13 Minutes of the general meeting of the
documenta foundation e. V., October 27, 1964,
Zentralarchiv für Deutsche und internationale
Kunstmarktforschung - ZADIK, A1, IV, 004.

14 Minutes of the general meeting of the
documenta foundation e. V., July 21, 1967,
Zentralarchiv für Deutsche und internationale
Kunstmarktforschung - ZADIK, A1, IV, 004.

15 Not all editions had been completed by June:
all available editions were put on sale, and later
editions were added as they were completed.

drawings, prints and other works of modern art are accessible to the general public; and (b) by publishing and distributing works of modern art.'[11] Before long, such ambiguity would cause quite a few headaches to the foundation's board of trustees – that is, the association's board of directors – and cast doubt on whether or not the foundation really was 'of general interest' and on the legitimacy of the tax advantages it claimed, arousing the misgivings of documenta GmbH itself, which ended up requesting that the foundation cease using its name if documenta was not explicitly mentioned in its statutes. To circumvent these problems, the foundation was forced to rectify and rephrase its mission statement: 'The aim of the association is to support international art exhibitions organised by documenta GmbH. For this purpose, the association may collect monetary donations and membership fees, accept works of art as donations in kind and, where appropriate, exploit them commercially through editions.'[12]

Despite the belatedness of the official registration, by the summer of 1964 the documenta foundation had already been active for some months. Herbert von Buttlar, archaeologist and curator at the Hessian Regional Museum in Kassel, had been appointed chairman; Hein Stünke, vice-chairman, and Christian Vowinckel, secretary.[13] They were later joined by Heinz Lemke, documenta's (part-time) managing director, and Andreas Vowinckel, who took over his brother's position before becoming managing director of the foundation.[14] With such a line-up, the foundation's close connection with documenta was assured, as von Buttlar and Lemke, former members of Club 53, were, together with Stünke, involved in the organisation of the exhibition. All three were members of the newly created documenta Board, and von Buttlar and Stünke were also members of the working committee specifically in charge of selecting the painting and sculpture for documenta III.

In the months prior to the opening of the exhibition, work being again subject to very tight production schedules, the team had gone all out to get 'Edition 64' ready for presentation in June: the first series of prints and multiples issued by the foundation, which were immediately put on sale in the area specially fitted out for this purpose on the second floor of the Fridericianum, a strategically situated spot right in the middle of the main visitor route. In addition to ten original works donated by as many artists, including Karl Hartung, Marino Marini, Ben Nicholson and Alicia Penalba, Edition 64 brought together pieces printed serially from originals ceded to the foundation by twenty-five artists.[15] Among these pieces were sculptures and three-dimensional objects by artists such as Alexander Calder, George Rickey and Henry Moore, as well as reliefs; but what abounded in particular

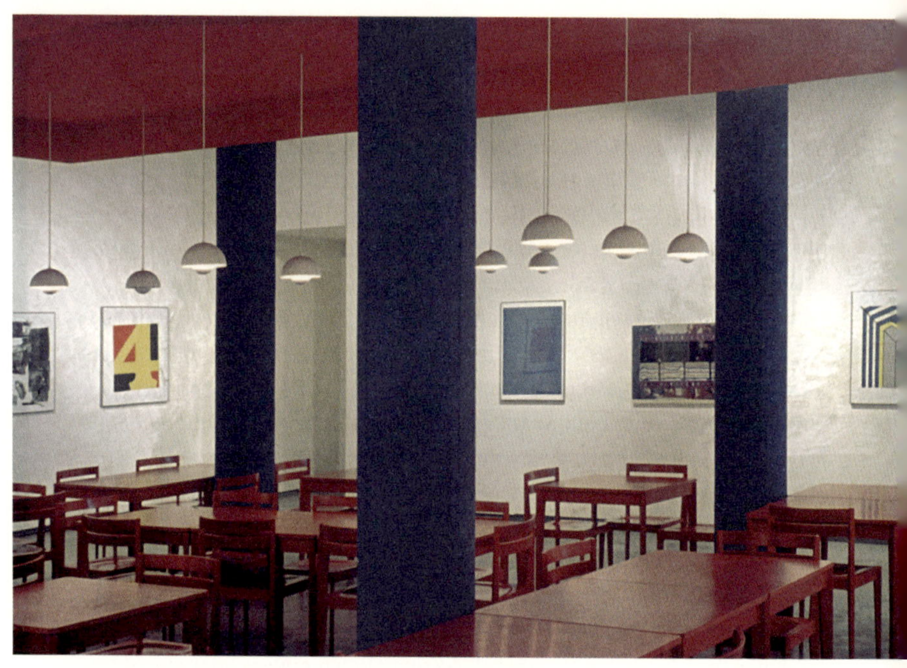

The cafeteria of documenta IV, decorated with some of the prints issued by the documenta foundation. Kassel, 1968. Left to right: Robert Rauschenberg, *Untitled*; Robert Indiana, *The German Four*; William Turnbull, *Untitled*; Joe Tilson, *The Software Chart*; and Nicholas Kruschenick, *documenta print* (all dated 1968). Photo: documenta archiv.

[16] A list of objects for sale, possibly drawn up in 1968, indicates that, of the twenty-nine artists who had made pieces for the 1964 Edition, seventeen had made prints, four had made reliefs, and eight had made sculptures or objects. In the 1968 Edition, in which thirty artists took part, the ratio was twenty-five prints versus seven objects or sculptures. (The discrepancy in the total figures is due to the fact that some artists made two pieces in different formats). Zentralarchiv für Deutsche und internationale Kunstmarktforschung - ZADIK, A1, IV, 002.

[17] Galerie Der Spiegel was responsible for the production of at least two of the pieces: *Scherben* by HAP Grieshaber and *Planetarische Volklore* by Victor Vasarely.

[18] 'Documenta: Kunst zu billigen Preisen'. In *Hessische Allgemeine*, 118, 1964, documenta archiv, AA, d03, 5.

[19] Arnold Bode, 'ars porcellana – Rosenthal Relief Reihe'. In Arnold Bode (ed.), *ars porcellana*. Cologne: Kölnischer Kunstverein, 1968.

[20] Andreas Vowinckel, op. cit., p. 22. My italics.

was graphic work – woodcuts, lithographs and some silkscreen prints.[16] With few exceptions, confined mostly to the three-dimensional pieces whose print runs were smaller, these works were produced in editions limited to 100 numbered and signed copies, often with the artists themselves overseeing the process to speed things up as much as possible.[17]

As production had started so late, when the time came to present the editions to the public in the summer of 1964, inevitably not all of them were finished. Nevertheless, sales again soared. 'The documenta management expects to achieve a net income of DM 200,000 in the first sales campaign,'[18] the press reported in June 1964. By the close of the exhibition, the foundation was in a position to contribute DM 170,000 to documenta, a sum a little below the initial optimistic expectations but certainly not negligible considering that the Federal Government's endowment to documenta III, channelled via the Federal Ministry of the Interior, had been DM 100,000. The experiment once again highlighted the commercial bonus that came with satisfying the appetite of a sector of the public eager to start their own art collection, with pieces costing for the most part under a thousand marks, motivated either by a real artistic interest, or by a desire to partake symbolically of the aesthetic and intellectual enjoyment associated with the upper classes, or by pure unadulterated consumerism. Whatever the buyers' individual motivations, they were certainly varied, just as the marketers' motivations must have been varied, too, and coloured by an array of different political sensibilities. Arnold Bode, for example, had often insisted on the informative and socialising potential which he believed lay in the distribution of art editions through the proper market channels: 'The production of books, for example, is a good parallel. It is the perfect opportunity to help art regain a greater self-understanding in society. And there is no need to fear that this would reduce the significance of the unique work of art. After all, Picasso's graphic work has not affected the value of his paintings.'[19] For Andreas Vowinckel, on the other hand, sales worked because of their appeal as capitalist exercises in individual freedom: 'Even on a small budget, art lovers found ways and means to acquire works of high quality in regard to aesthetics, form and content, and guided by their own tastes, *without any state or social paternalism.*'[20]

However, not everyone shared this satisfaction about the sales success of Edition 64. Very soon, gallery owners in the Federal Republic began to raise suspicions about a practice which they felt was damaging their commercial interests. The foundation knew they had not welcomed the experiment and had mentioned this cursorily at the board meetings in the summer of 1964, as the minutes of the meetings show: 'The German

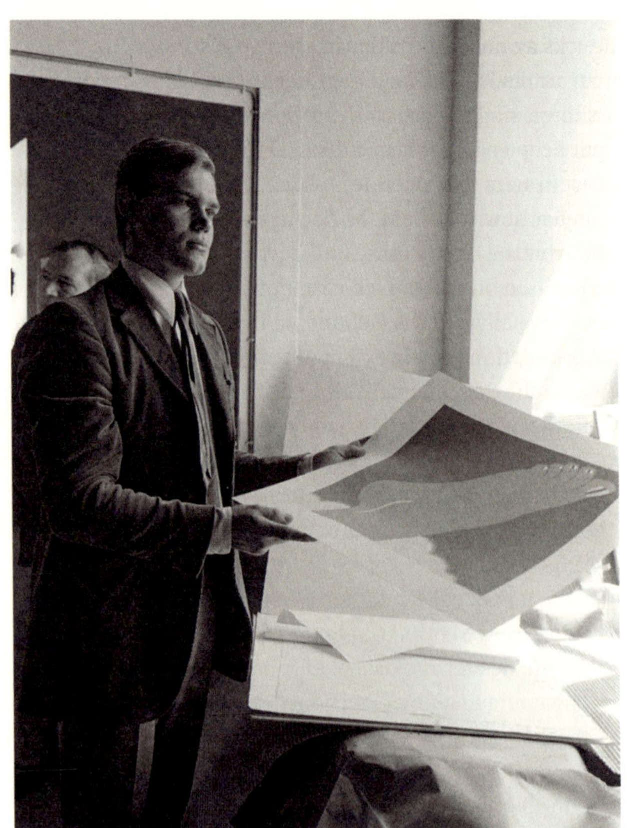

Andreas Vowinckel in the stand where the prints
and multiples issued by the documenta foundation
were on sale during documenta IV, 1968. In the
foreground, *Untitled*, by Tom Wesselmann, 1968.
Photo: Angelika Platen.

[21] Minutes of the general meeting of the
documenta foundation e. V., July 24, 1964,
Zentralarchiv für Deutsche und internationale
Kunstmarktforschung - ZADIK, AI, IV, 004.

[22] Andreas Vowinckel, op. cit., p. 23.

[23] Minutes of the general meeting
of the documenta foundation
e.V., July 21, 1967, op. cit.

[24] Andreas Vowinckel, op. cit., p. 25.

galleries' fierce attacks against this initiative are also discussed, and it is agreed that German art dealers, instead of protesting, should support it, since after all, by showcasing the artists the galleries represent, the latter benefit from the publicity given to these artists. One might be so bold as to ask German art dealers to cooperate.'[21] Their attitude towards the protests is a sign of just how confident the documenta foundation was about its raison d'être at the close of the third edition of the exhibition, and about its own position on the game board, not only in relation to the art market, but above all vis-à-vis documenta itself: 'It was no longer possible to see the foundation merely as a sponsor that provided as much funding as possible for the documenta exhibitions, as Arnold Bode had originally wished. Rather, the foundation had become a partner whose statutory task was to organise exhibitions of its own.'[22] It would take a few more years before it became clear if this confidence was justified or if it was just part of the commercial effervescence surrounding the foundation in the summer of 1964.

After the organisational and fundraising heyday of documenta III, the foundation's activity slowed over the next three years, as did the pace of its board meetings. As neither the dates nor the content of documenta IV (which was once again hanging by a thread due to money problems) had yet been defined, the foundation fell into a kind of lethargy during which only a few general decisions were made, such as not admitting any more members (the foundation's board and the members of the association were practically the same small group of people), and working only with artists invited to exhibit at documenta for upcoming editions.[23] The foundation emerged from this lethargy with renewed vigour in 1967, ready to begin work not only on the editions for 1968, but also on a more ambitious project: *Ambiente*, a section 'of its own' within the general exhibition, the realisation of which was almost a matter of justice for the foundation: 'Even though this certainly did not chime with the intentions of Arnold Bode, who as exhibition director continued to claim overall planning and responsibility for himself, the foundation not only *could*, but *must* be granted such a framework of action if it was to remain involved in the financing of documenta and participate in it accordingly.'[24] Some of the most spectacular and eye-catching projects of documenta 1968 were held in *Ambiente*: besides *Projekt Geldmacher Mariotti*, it was here that Christo presented his gigantic vertical balloon, *5,000 Cubic Meter Package*, which he partly financed out of his own pocket. After repeated attempts, the balloon only managed to remain upright in the air for a few hours which, nonetheless, was enough for it to be immortalised in a great many

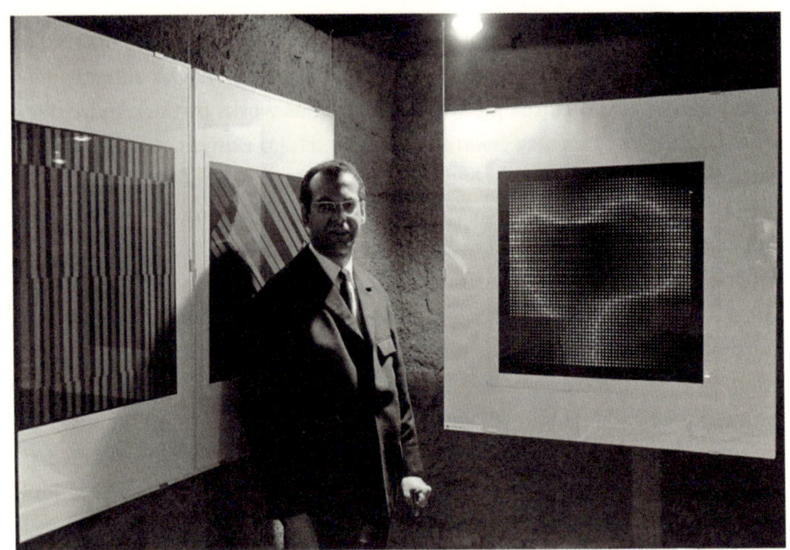

Almir Mavignier next to one of his prints, documenta IV, 1968.
Photo: Angelika Platen.

25 Willi Bongard, 'Gute Geschäfte mit Grafik'. In *Die Zeit*, 33, 1968, p. 28, documenta archiv, AA, d04, 12. It should not be forgotten that the editor of the news section of the art market in *Die Zeit* was Willi Bongard, a member of the working committee for communication at documenta IV and a firm advocate of the commercial potential of editions and multiples.

photographs and etch itself forever on to the visual memory of documenta
IV. Also part of *Ambiente* were Edward Kienholz's installation *Roxy's* and
Lucas Samaras's mirrored glass cube, as well as works by Carl Andre,
Enrico Castellani, Chryssa, Gianni Colombo, Hugo Demarco, Dan Flavin,
Lucio Fontana, Robert Rauschenberg, Martial Raysse and Tony Smith.

The foundation's activity was not limited to financing this section,
but also included the presentation and sale of 'Edition 68', a new batch of
artists' editions that would again yield juicy profits. Once more, the press
was keen to underline the success of the event and reveal which were the
most sought-after works: 'The investment of the documenta foundation,
whose offer of graphic work serves to finance the costly *Ambiente*
programme of documenta IV, seems to be paying off. The interest shown
by visitors to Kassel – more than 70,000 so far – is greater than expected,
even though most of the prints and objects for sale are examples of avant-
garde art rather than works by established artists. Andreas Vowinckel, the
managing director of the foundation, which has its office in the rooms of the
Fridericianum in Kassel, was already able to record sales of over a quarter of
a million marks by last weekend. A colour serigraph by the American artist
Kenneth Noland proved to be the best seller. Despite its relatively high price
of DM 500, eighty copies have already been sold out of a total edition of one
hundred and fifty. In second place was a serigraph by the French *nouveau
realiste* Arman, of which two-thirds of the available edition of 75 copies
were reported as sold at a price of DM 200. Also particularly in demand
were lithographs and serigraphs by Robert Indiana, Nicholas Krushenik,
Tom Wesselmann and Robert Rauschenberg, as well as small sculptures by
George Rickey and wooden objects by Tony Smith.'[25]

The foundation's methodology for producing this edition had
changed slightly, not so much on its own initiative as simply out of a need
to adapt. Art galleries, whose economic might – and therefore influence –
had been growing steadily since the early 1960s, were increasingly playing
the role of the artists' exclusive representatives, making it difficult not to
involve them in some way in the deals. In contrast to Edition 64, where it
had almost always been the artists who had ceded their originals without
receiving any benefit in return, in this new edition it was agreed that a part
of the print run of each edition would be handed over to their galleries,
effectively giving them financial compensation of a kind for their part in
mediating between artists and the foundation, facilitating production and
so on. The relationship between the publishing entity and its 'donors',
who were no longer necessarily the creators but their representatives on
the market and whose motivations were perhaps less altruistic and more

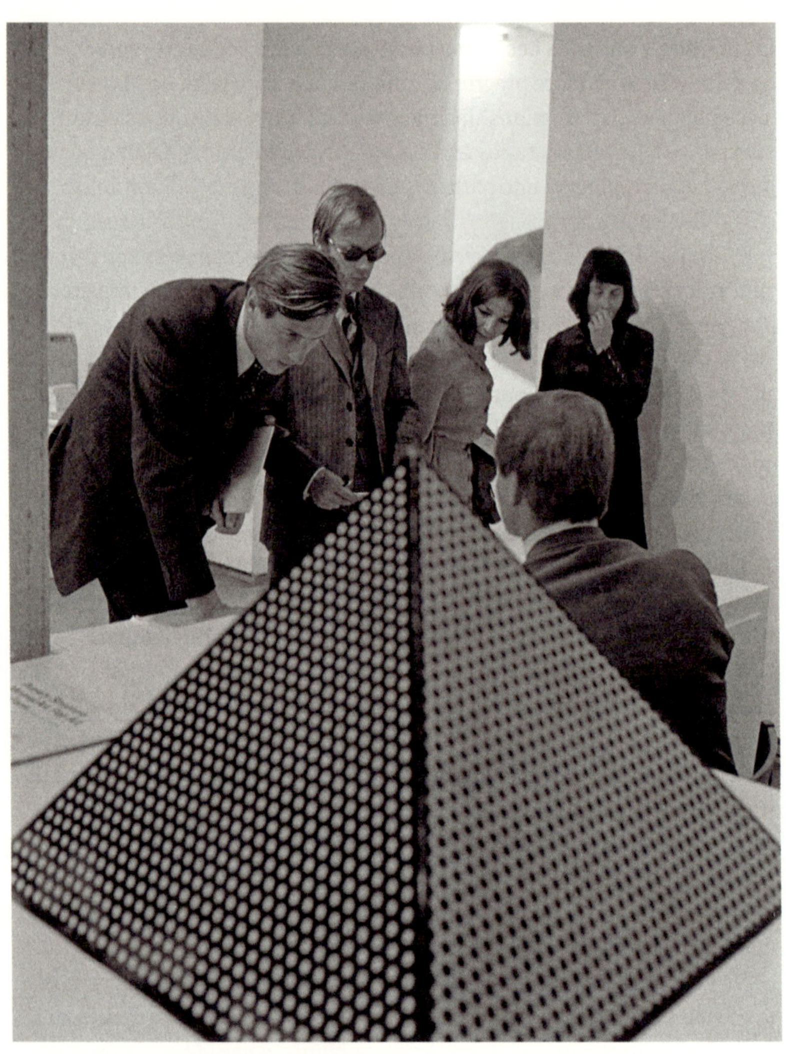

Stand where the prints and multiples issued by
the documenta foundation were on sale during
documenta IV, 1968. Left, Rudolf Zwirner; in the
foreground, *Pyramid*, by Roy Lichtenstein, 1968.
Photo: Angelika Platen.

[26] Silkscreen on thin cardboard, 50 cm base
x 37 cm height, 2 inks, printed at Fine
Creation Inc., New York, with the collaboration
of Charles Cardinale for the printing.

[27] Mary Lee Corlett (ed.), *The Prints of Roy
Lichtenstein: A Catalogue Raisonné
1948-1993*. New York: National Gallery
of Art / Hudson Hills, 1994, p. 94.

commercial, was thus becoming professionalised. Therefore, agreements generally became more pragmatic, and because they were no longer based on personal relationships their terms were not always as clear to all involved. The vicissitudes endured in the production of Lichtenstein's *Pyramid*, undoubtedly one of the most striking items in Edition 68, is certainly a case in point.

In 1961, Roy Lichtenstein had begun to employ a manipulated version of the dot screen, invented by the American illustrator and printer Ben Day, which mass media such as comics, newspapers and billboards had been using since the 1950s. Thanks to the technical characteristics of dot screening, certain combinations of dots in the basic colours – red, black, blue, yellow on white – could be printed in such a way as to trick the eye, making it see secondary colours and shading, an effect that could not be achieved on the cheap papers typically used for this type of publication. In one of his characteristic gestures of appropriating pop culture images, Lichtenstein began to manipulate and modify this dot pattern until it became one of the distinguishing graphic resources of his painting and sculpture. *Pyramid*, a silkscreen print that becomes a three-dimensional object when appropriately folded,[26] employs this technique, but the dots are enlarged almost disproportionately. The artist would later explain that he had originally devised the prototype of the pyramid to use in his studio as a prop to help him calculate the proportions of one of his paintings, but later decided to transform it into a multiple and continue using the motif in different paintings and prints.

Records relating to Edition 68 show that Lichtenstein was one of the artists the foundation had wished to invite from the start. But when Leo Castelli, his gallerist at the time, was approached by the foundation, he objected that there was not enough time to conceive a new multiple and proposed that Kassel dispose of several copies of *Pyramid*, the multiple the artist had just produced in collaboration with his gallery. It is not clear if Lichtenstein knew of this agreement between Castelli and the foundation, but it seems plausible that it was an internal decision made without his knowledge. In any case, the information available about the piece is confusing. The corresponding catalogue raisonné of Roy Lichtenstein's graphic work[27] makes no mention or reference to the documenta foundation. It states that the plan was to make a print run of 300 copies, but the artist recalled that the freshly printed copies had not been left to dry properly before being stacked, meaning that only 50 or 100 could be used. The documenta foundation's surviving lists and the brochures published to promote its editions always include *Pyramid*; but apart from the error

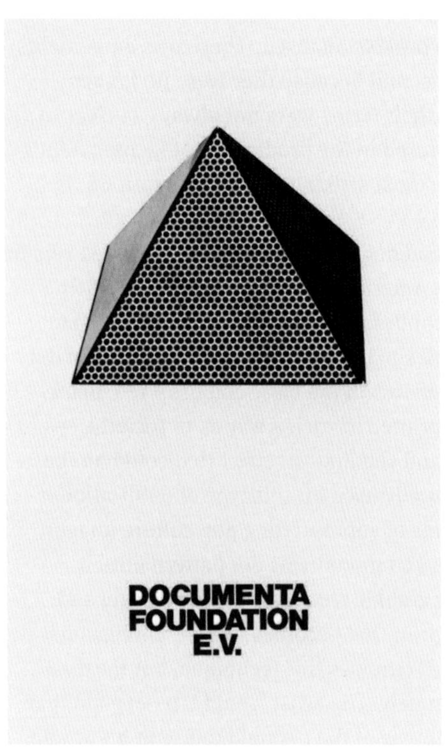

documenta foundation [brochure], 1977.

regarding the printing technique used (it says it was offset printed when it is a serigraph), they consistently state that the print run of this multiple was 300 signed and numbered copies.

Such discrepancies certainly suggest something of a communication problem with the artist. In the absence of detailed documentation about each and every one of the pieces comprising Edition 68, it is difficult to say how much the artists involved knew about the final destination of their pieces, or what the documenta foundation's role was in their production. But one way or another, the irrefutable fact remains that, in the preparations for Edition 68, gallery owners had acquired a relevance that they did not have in 1964. Subsequent events would show that the documenta foundation, perhaps blinded by the support it received from its significant income, and despite having an art market professional of Hein Stünke's standing and experience in its ranks, did not seem able to appreciate this change of model to its full extent.

The Rosenthal Relief Series

[1] Daniel Spoerri, letter to Joseph Albers, 1959,
quoted by Katerina Vatsella, op. cit., p. 37.

[2] Hans Eckstein, 'Unsere Gegenstände –
Zur Eröffnung der Design-Documenta'.
In *form*, no. 27, 1964, p. 2.

The confusion surrounding its history is not the only reason why *Pyramid* stands out among all the multiples and prints issued for Edition 64 and Edition 68. Lichtenstein's piece is, along with Michael Tyzack's *Kite*, one of the few that truly conform to the idea of the 'multiple' postulated by Daniel Spoerri in the late 1950s, i.e. a 'multiplied original work'[1] where form is neither entirely stable nor fixed. For the most part, the documenta foundation's editions, which were above all prints and small objects, were scarcely experimental or innovative in this regard. Rather, they fitted into the established tradition of multiplication or seriality that dates back to the time of Dürer, at the turn of the sixteenth century, and was well known to artists, Kunstvereine, galleries, and the public. The most experimental area of the documenta foundation's publishing initiative lay not in any of these pieces, but in a different project started not by the foundation's members, but by Arnold Bode himself: the Rosenthal Relief Series.

One of the many facets of Arnold Bode's professional life was his intense activity in industrial and interior design. Bode was consequently very well connected with industrial manufacturing, something that would stand him in excellent stead when the documenta exhibition project took off. In 1955, even though success was still anything but assured, a handful of industrialists did not hesitate to join the group of key supporters of the documenta enterprise. They helped not only with money, but also with assistance in kind. Indeed, the recourse to materials and methods used in industrial production still stands out today as one of the characteristic features of the carefully designed display sets that Bode created for the first four documentas. Given this background of close partnerships with industrial manufacturers, it was entirely congruous that in 1964 documenta should feature, for the first time, an exhibition of graphic and industrial design, which included machines and engineering projects by Marcello Nizzoi, Eliot Noyes and Klaus Flesche alongside furniture by Mies van der Rohe, Arne Jacobsen, Charles Eams and Gerrit Rietveld.[2] And it was also predictable that Bode's far-reaching ideas would end up involving some of his industrial friends in ways that transcended mere donations. Rosenthal AG's role in the production of editions for the documenta foundation was just one such instance.

The porcelain manufacturer Rosenthal had developed in parallel with that of the Jewish family from which its name derived. In 1879, the first Philipp Rosenthal, then aged twenty-four, was back in Germany after an adventurous period in America and setting up a modest workshop specialising in hand-painted porcelain, a business he knew well since his father had been a crockery salesman all his life. Established in Selb, a small

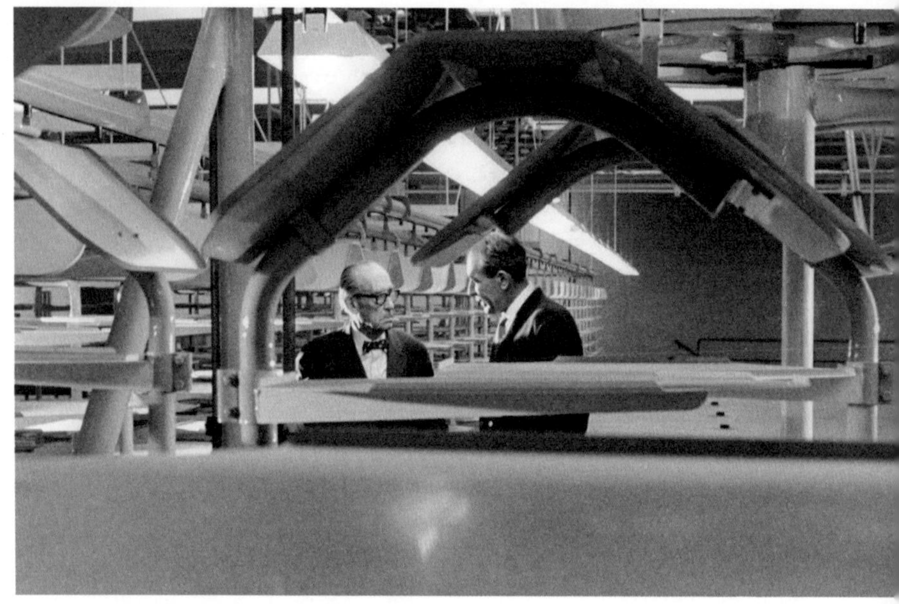

Walther Gropius and Philip Rosenthal in conversation
at the porcelain factory in Rothbühl, ca. 1968.
Photo: Porzellanikon Museum Archive.

[3] Philip Rosenthal, quoted in Hermann
Schreiber, 'Reicher Junge, armer Hund'. In
Dieter Honisch et al. (eds.), *Die Rosenthal
Story*. Düsseldorf: Econ Verlag, 1980, p. 32.

town in southern Germany with a long history in porcelain manufacturing, the workshop proved to be a success, and over the decades the company expanded, soon branching out into industrial manufacturing as its crockery and household items sought to satisfy an ever-increasing demand from private clients. In time, Philipp Rosenthal became a wealthy industrialist and businessman.

In 1934, however, things went seriously awry. The prosperous businessman, who had converted to Protestantism years earlier and married a Catholic, was no longer 'the German Rosenthal' but 'the Jewish Rosenthal' and was forced to step down as company director as a result of one of the numerous 'Aryanisation' campaings the Nazis were implementing all over Germany. Shortly afterwards, he and all his family members were required to sell their shares.

Philipp Rosenthal died in 1937, old and impoverished, while his former company, now in Nazi hands, continued to operate. But after the war, in 1947, Rosenthal's only son, also named Philip and a graduate of Politics, Economics and Philosophy from Oxford University, returned from England to Germany to reclaim his father's property. In 1950, he joined the company as head of advertising, moving to head of design in 1952 and taking over the sales department in 1954, and in 1958 was appointed company chairman, a position he held until 1981 with only one interruption of two years during which he pursued a brief career in politics as an elected member of parliament for the Social Democratic Party.

Cultured, cosmopolitan, charismatic and a clear risk-taker, Philip Rosenthal instinctively felt that to expand the company he would have to adopt strategies that combined technical research and artistic creativity. 'My skills lie only in finding the best people in design, art, advertising, technology and sales, and of course bringing them all together,' he explained in 1979.[3] Under his leadership, the porcelain company collaborated with more than a hundred product designers – men and women – from all over the world who, along with engineers and artists from various disciplines and other in-house professionals, would regularly meet on the company premises to exchange ideas, broaden horizons and further personal contacts.

Just as he was convinced by the benefits of combining art and design – creative freedom and product design – Rosenthal also believed that a good working environment could improve employees' quality of life. He therefore did not hesitate to request Walter Gropius's cooperation when it came to designing a new porcelain factory in Rothbühl and a glass foundry in Amberg, where cutting-edge technical advances and optimum environmental

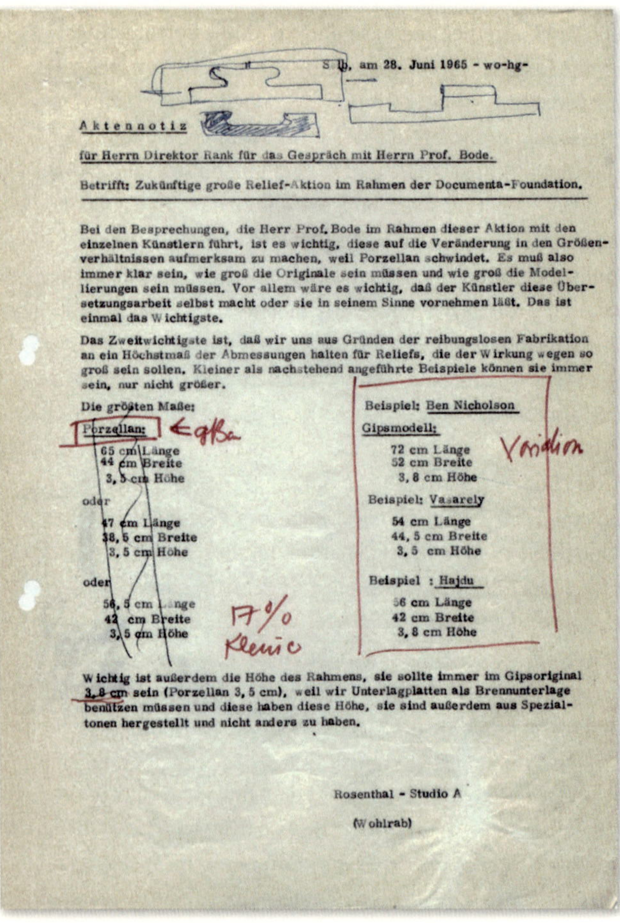

Selb, am 28. Juni 1965 - wo-hg-

A k t e n n o t i z

für Herrn Direktor Rank für das Gespräch mit Herrn Prof. Bode.

Betrifft: Zukünftige große Relief-Aktion im Rahmen der Documenta-Foundation.

Bei den Besprechungen, die Herr Prof. Bode im Rahmen dieser Aktion mit den einzelnen Künstlern führt, ist es wichtig, diese auf die Veränderung in den Größenverhältnissen aufmerksam zu machen, weil Porzellan schwindet. Es muß also immer klar sein, wie groß die Originale sein müssen und wie groß die Modellierungen sein müssen. Vor allem wäre es wichtig, daß der Künstler diese Übersetzungsarbeit selbst macht oder sie in seinem Sinne vornehmen läßt. Das ist einmal das Wichtigste.

Das Zweitwichtigste ist, daß wir uns aus Gründen der reibungslosen Fabrikation an ein Höchstmaß der Abmessungen halten für Reliefs, die der Wirkung wegen so groß sein sollen. Kleiner als nachstehend angeführte Beispiele können sie immer sein, nur nicht größer.

Die größten Maße:

Porzellan:

65 cm Länge
44 cm Breite
3, 5 cm Höhe

oder

47 cm Länge
38, 5 cm Breite
3, 5 cm Höhe

oder

56, 5 cm Länge
42 cm Breite
3, 5 cm Höhe

Beispiel: Ben Nicholson

Gipsmodell:

72 cm Länge
52 cm Breite
3, 8 cm Höhe

Beispiel: Vasarely

54 cm Länge
44, 5 cm Breite
3, 5 cm Höhe

Beispiel : Hajdu

56 cm Länge
42 cm Breite
3, 8 cm Höhe

Wichtig ist außerdem die Höhe des Rahmens, sie sollte immer im Gipsoriginal 3,8 cm sein (Porzellan 3, 5 cm), weil wir Unterlagplatten als Brennunterlage benützen müssen und diese haben diese Höhe, sie sind außerdem aus Spezialtonen hergestellt und nicht anders zu haben.

Rosenthal - Studio A

(Wohlrab)

Typed note, June 28, 1965, with instructions from Rosenthal technicians informing the artists of the Relief Series of the changes the porcelain undergoes during firing. Handwritten annotations in red by Arnold Bode. Source: Kölnischer Stadtarchiv.

4 Thanks to his friendship with Rosenthal, Gropius would also develop the so-called *Gropius Plan* for the transformation of the urban layout of Selb. See Walther Gropius und The Architects Collaborative [TAC], *Town Plan for the Development of Selb: Town Planning by Walter Gropius and The Architects Collaborative, Inc., Traffic Planning by Kurt Leibbrand and Verkehrs- und Industrieplanung GmbH.* Cambridge, Mass.: MIT Press, 1969.

5 The mansion, built in 1748, had been acquired by the company in 1953.

6 Of particular interest is the decoration that HAP Grieshaber created for the foyer, which has survived to this day.

7 The third line of work was the *Studio Line*, which brought avant-garde design to everyday objects. See Bernd Fritz, 'Limitierte Kunst bei Rosenthal'. In *Mit Kunst Leben. Hommage Philip Rosenthal.* Selb: Rosenthal AG, 2003.

conditions should work together and harmonise with the surroundings. Opened in 1967, the Rothbühl factory would be the last building planned and personally supervised by Walter Gropius, who died in 1969, only a few months before the inauguration of the glass foundry. Embedded in the landscape like a sculpture, the complex includes a greenhouse and a two-storey *Feierabendhaus* – an 'after-work house' – equipped with a canteen, ping-pong tables and a library. Gropius and Rosenthal's collaboration over the Rothbühl factory grew into a friendship, sowing the seeds of the *TAC* porcelain set that Gropius designed with his studio, The Architects' Collaborative, and which is still in production today.[4]

A similar sense of social responsibility combined with an interest in artistic creation informed many other actions Rosenthal undertook. In 1973, the Italian artist Otto Piene was asked to create a colourful mural covering the façade of the old porcelain factory in Selb. From 1956 to the 1970s, the Erkersreuth mansion, where Philipp Rosenthal senior established his first business and Philip Rosenthal junior and part of his team took up residence,[5] was the setting for almost four hundred cultural events organised by the company, including exhibitions (Henry Moore, Victor Vasarely), theatrical performances (Marcel Marceau and the Prague Black Theatre), concerts (Yehudi Menuhin, Louis Armstrong), dance performances (Oskar Schlemmer's Triadic Ballet) and literary evenings, with Ernst Jünger reading Bertolt Brecht and Günther Grass reading himself, among others.

While Rosenthal did invite some artists to create pieces in situ at Erkersreuth,[6] the collaborations to which he was partial would focus mainly on the production of porcelain, for two of the company's three production lines required their input:[7] for the design of objects for practical use such as plates, vases, tea and coffee sets, cutlery and even furniture on the one hand; and the various sets of decorative objects Rosenthal produced in limited series on the other. One of these was the series of experimental reliefs made for the documenta foundation.

The idea of using porcelain as an artistic material was certainly not new. Already in the nineteenth century, porcelain pieces had inspired various artists, and at the beginning of the twentieth century 'artistic' porcelain gained increasing renown in Central European countries, although its design remained somewhat conventional. In 1910, Philipp Rosenthal senior had opened an 'art department' for ornamental porcelains in his Selb factory. Philip junior, in turn, rather than merely commissioning artists to produce a particular piece, put the material – porcelain – and the production resources at artists' complete disposal so they could decide for themselves what form their experiments and trials should take.

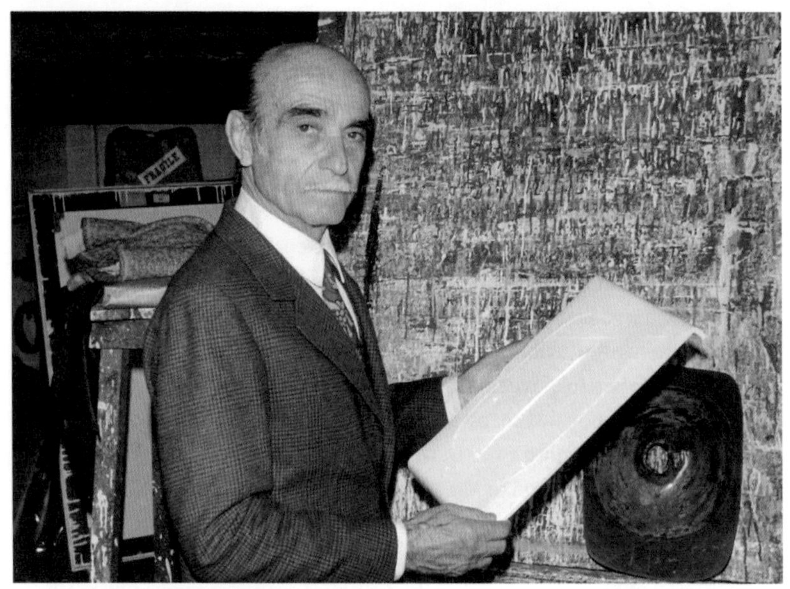

Lucio Fontana with two of his reliefs
for the Rosenthal Series, ca. 1968.
Photo: Porzellanikon Museum Archive.

[8] Henry-Pierre Fourest, *Die europäische Keramik. Porzellan - Steingut - Fayence.* Freiburg: Herder, 1983, p. 377.

[9] Together with Max Bill, Otl Aicher and Inge Aicher-Scholl were co-founders of the Ulm School of Design [Hochschule für Gestaltung Ulm], which was in operation from 1953 to 1968.

To contextualise the Rosenthal Relief Series, it is essential to understand the philosophy of the company Rosenthal AG, which was based on how Philip Rosenthal conceived the relationship between fine art and design. In his view, the company's mission was to recover the lost cultural significance of porcelain as a material, not by imitating styles, but by collaborating with artists and designers of the present day.[8] This philosophy was framed within a long-standing debate which, both in theory and in practice, called into play the hierarchy that subordinates the applied arts to fine art, the tension between ornamentation and art, and the relationship between mass production and artisanal handicraft: in short, the variables of the correspondence between form and function. Ever since the nineteenth century there had been successive attempts to liberate the applied arts from their subordination to 'art for art's sake' and broaden the concept of 'artwork' to encompass objects whose primary purpose was not aesthetic but practical. William Morris and the Arts and Crafts movement in England had leaned in this direction, while modernist architecture incorporated ornamentation as one of its characteristic elements. But it was not until 1900 and the spread of industrialisation that the debate became truly relevant. In Germany, the discussion was led by the Deutsche Werkbund, a mixed association of architects, artists and industrialists founded in 1907 by the architect Hermann Muthesius with the aim of combining industrial techniques of mass production with traditional crafts to improve the country's commercial competitiveness. Walter Gropius was a member of the Werkbund, which inspired the founding principles of a project he would start in 1919: the Staatliche Bauhaus Weimar, arguably the most legendary pedagogical experiment in the entire history of art. At the Bauhaus School, art and craft were on the same hierarchical level, although classes were given by artists and not artisans. Moreover, in contrast with traditional schools that taught painting, sculpture or design, students were expected to draw on a basic knowledge of materials and principles to design and create in all spheres of existence. Some years after World War II, taking the Bauhaus as a model, former student Max Bill founded the Ulm School of Design,[9] another pedagogical initiative offering artists and designers the same practical training and principles.

If these were the debates informing the field of design, in art the Secession movements led by artists around the turn of the century (in 1892 in Munich, 1897 in Vienna, and 1898 in Berlin) caused classical artistic genres – painting and sculpture – to spill over into architecture and the design of interiors, jewellery, furniture and everyday objects, fostering a more intense relationship between fine art and the applied arts. After the

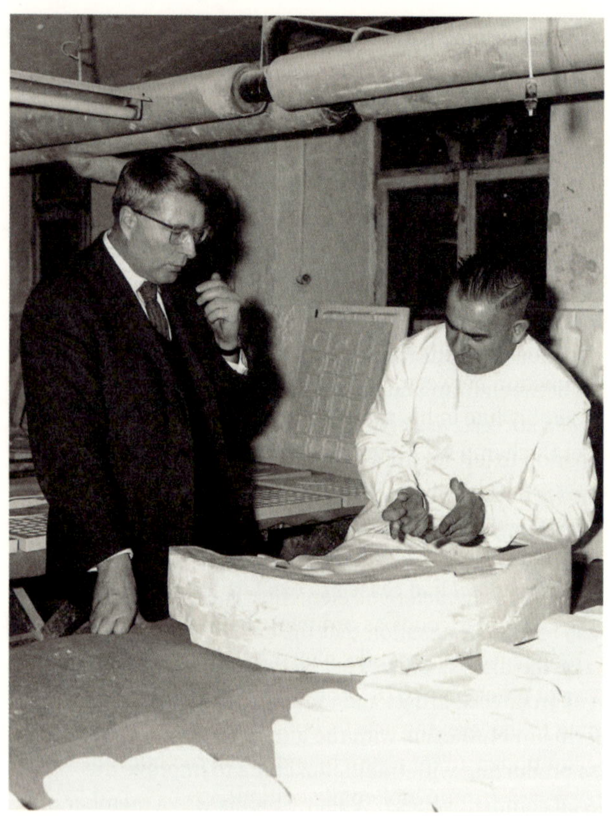

Wilhelm Loth working with a Rosenthal technician, ca. 1968.
Photo: Porzellanikon Museum Archive.

10 Heiner Georgsdorf (ed.), *Arnold Bode,
Schriften und Gespräche*. Kassel
and Frankfurt: documenta archiv and
Siebenhaar Verlag, 2007, p. 26 ff.

11 Ibid., p. 69 ff.

war, Arnold Bode would become part of a movement in the Hessian region that advocated the revival of the classical Secessions,[10] although it must be noted that even in spite of his strong defence of the value of design, he would never fully overcome the system of hierarchies: in his view, the genre that should lead the breakthrough into modernity was painting, from where modernity would extend to the other arts.[11]

In the artistic avant-gardes, in turn, the crossover of utilitarian objects and artwork was widespread from the beginning of the twentieth century. Via the technique of collage, Dada had already begun to integrate industrially manufactured utensils into works of art, blurring the hierarchical distinction between the two. While Henry Ford was introducing the assembly line in his car factories on the other side of the Atlantic, Marcel Duchamp was coining the idea of the 'readymade', whereby any everyday object, manufactured or not, could be transformed into a work of art merely by the artist's express declaration. The readymade thus effectively fulminated the distinction between original work and reproduction since the *original* had ceased to exist. In the 1950s, Pop art began transforming consumer goods as ordinary and banal as a can of soup or a packet of washing powder into works of art. And at around the same time, in the practice of pioneers like Dieter Roth and Edward Ruscha, a new genre was beginning to emerge: the artist's book, whose main feature was its potential to be multiplied ad infinitum by industrial methods, unlike the exquisite *livres de peintre* and bibliophile editions so cherished by Hein and Eva Stünke in their Galerie Der Spiegel. The motivations of Roth, Ruscha and other artists who created artists' books were not only aesthetic but political too: books offered creators the chance to circumvent the limitations of the art market and reach a much wider public, since, at least in theory, distribution was greater – and more horizontal – than it could ever be for original artworks.

These ideas were in the air in the 1960s and 70s, during Rosenthal's 'golden age' in Selb, when fine artists were constantly being invited to participate in various processes of porcelain production and the company was catering for its local community with a cultural programme on a par with the best urban centres of the time. One staff member in particular proved key in ensuring the exquisite quality of this programme of activities, while simultaneously acting as a 'conveyor belt' between the porcelain company and contemporary reflections permeating art and design. This man was none other than the visual poet Eugen Gomringer, who worked for Philip Rosenthal as head of cultural relations from 1967 – just before documenta IV – to 1985.

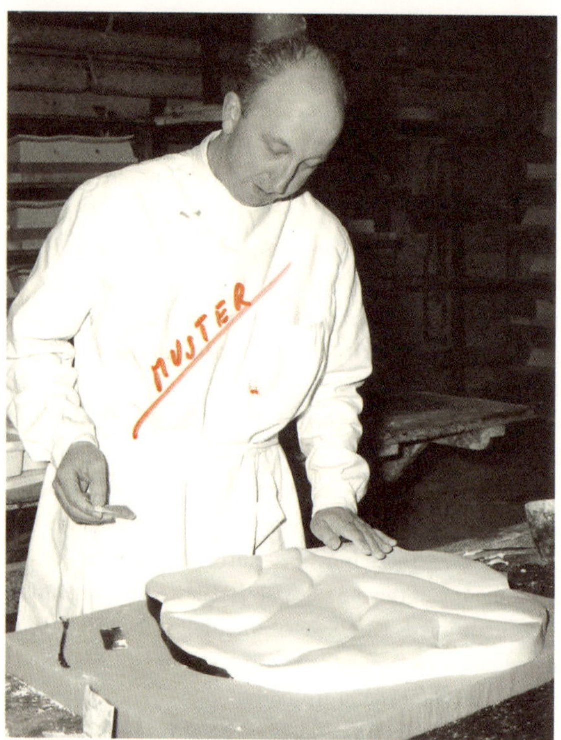

Emil Cimiotti working on his relief in the Rosenthal factory, ca. 1968.
Photo: Porzellanikon Museum Archive.

12 Eugen Gomringer, 'Die dritte Haut.
Eine Hommage an Unternehmer Philip
Rosenthal'. In *Mit Kunst Leben. Hommage
Philip Rosenthal*, op. cit., p. 25.

Eugen Gomringer, the son of a Swiss father and a Bolivian mother, was born in Bolivia in 1925 and brought up by his grandparents in Switzerland, where, after a brief stint in the army, he studied art history and economics. His penchant for poetic experimentation manifested itself early and would remain constant throughout his life. As early as 1953, he founded the magazine *Spirale*, together with the artists Dieter Roth and Marcel Wyss, which would run for eleven years. In 1959, he was one of the authors of the first Edition MAT series of multiples, launched by his friend Daniel Spoerri, and in 1960 he published his own collection of books entitled *Poesía Concreta Heraus* [Concrete Poetry Heraus], which established him as the European 'father' of concrete poetry, a sub-genre halfway between literature and the visual arts that plays with the materiality of language, typography and page surface as its main creative elements.

Since it cannot have been easy to make a living from poetry, let alone experimental poetry, as a young man Eugen Gomringer worked as an office assistant, a career move that would take him very close to the hotbed of the conceptual revolution happening in the field of industrial design. In 1954, he became Max Bill's secretary at the Ulm School, where he stayed for three years before being made director of the Swiss Werkbund, a post he held until 1967, when Philip Rosenthal hired him as head of cultural relations for his company. Given Gomringer's close relationship with artists and the art world, as well as his previous involvement in initiatives of such significance to the transformation of design, his collaboration greatly enriched the working and cultural environment which Rosenthal aspired to develop. Years later, Gomringer would recall how that particular creative crossroads came about: 'For a long time artists in Selb lived a kind of "club life", with a good mix of young and old people, rather like the Bauhaus festivals in Dessau or the Ulm College of Design. Speaking of Ulm: the design innovations that Philip Rosenthal encouraged showed certain parallels with those carried out by Max Bill and his team at the legendary design centre in Ulm. Seen with the benefit of hindsight, the differences between the rational design principles of the Ulmers and the emotional design of the 'porcelainers' introduced two much-needed additions.'[12]

Meanwhile, Arnold Bode and Philip Rosenthal had met in Kassel in 1959 at documenta II, instantly seeing eye to eye, and it was not long before Bode began working with Rosenthal as a consultant. Dietrich Müller, who held various positions of responsibility in the company before his appointment as chairman in the 1980s, replacing Philip Rosenthal, recalls Bode's role in the company: 'When I started as head of product development at Rosenthal AG in 1964, production of the reliefs for the documenta

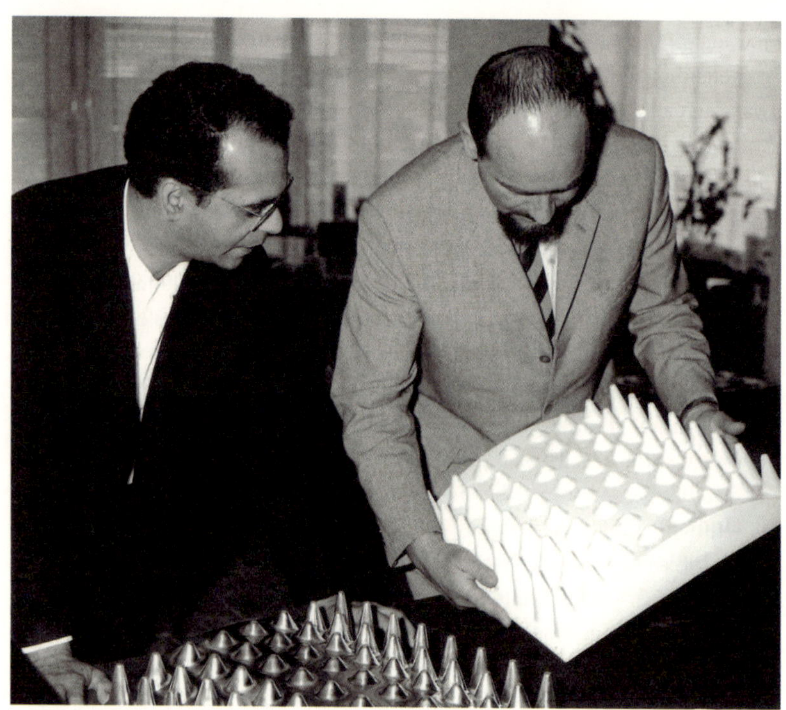

Almil Mavignier with a technician in the Rosenthal factory, ca. 1968.
Photo: Porzellanikon Museum Archive.

[13] Dietrich Müller, email to the author, 2021. Müller also clarified that the motivation for the trip to Granada had been to study the decoration of the Alhambra.

[14] Arnold Bode, 'ars porcellana – Rosenthal Relief Reihe', op. cit.

foundation had just concluded. The team was talking about how the
dimensions of the pieces had presented a technical challenge... The initiative
was seen as a way of supporting Arnold Bode's documenta, but everyone
was quite happy that the collaboration had, for the time being, come to an
end. It wasn't considered necessary to highlight this project in the brand's
marketing campaigns, but contact with Arnold Bode was maintained and
highly valued. Professor Bode went on to become a member of Rosenthal's
international panel, composed of seven people, and from then on came to
Selb quite regularly, three or four times a year, to oversee the development
of the collection. My relationship with him was very cordial. It was at one of
our artistic meetings, in Granada in 1964,[13] that Bode came up with the idea
of continuing the project for the documenta foundation with more reliefs,
and he himself contacted all the artists involved'.

The first round of reliefs had been executed shortly before the 1964
documenta, when, as Arnold Bode recalled, 'there was talk of extending
the foundation's graphic editions to include sculpture. At that time, still
stuck as we were in an analogy with painters' graphic work, we had the
idea of asking artists to make reliefs that could be serially produced.
Porcelain was a suitable material for this, on the one hand because it
has something precious about it, it is sensual and attractive to the touch
without being expensive; and on the other because Philip Rosenthal was
interested in working with good artists to help bring about a renaissance
of porcelain sculpture'.[14] The bulk of the series, in which a total of
twenty-two artists took part, of whom only one was a woman (Nele,
Arnold Bode's daughter), would be executed in the second half of 1965 for
presentation at documenta IV.

Despite the initial idea that the series should be composed of reliefs,
not all of the pieces in the Rosenthal Relief Series were two-dimensional:
Henry Moore, Lucio Fontana and Ferdinand Ris conceived free-standing,
three-dimensional objects. The most complex collaborations were with Ben
Nicholson, who repeatedly judged the porcelain factory's proofs of his piece
to be inaccurate, and Henry Moore. The English sculptor, who had initially
declined Bode's invitation, accepted on the condition that his piece would
not be a relief but a sculpture. Ironically, although the point of the project
was to experiment with reproducibility, Moore's works for the series, *Moon
Head* (1964) and *Three Way Ring* (1966), were executed according to the
convention of bronze editions, that is, in a limited series of six. Walther
Stürmer, then head of development at Rosenthal, later recalled: 'To my
surprise, Henry Moore wanted to cover *Moon Sculpture* in a gold patina
so that the white porcelain wouldn't be visible at all. [...] In the end he

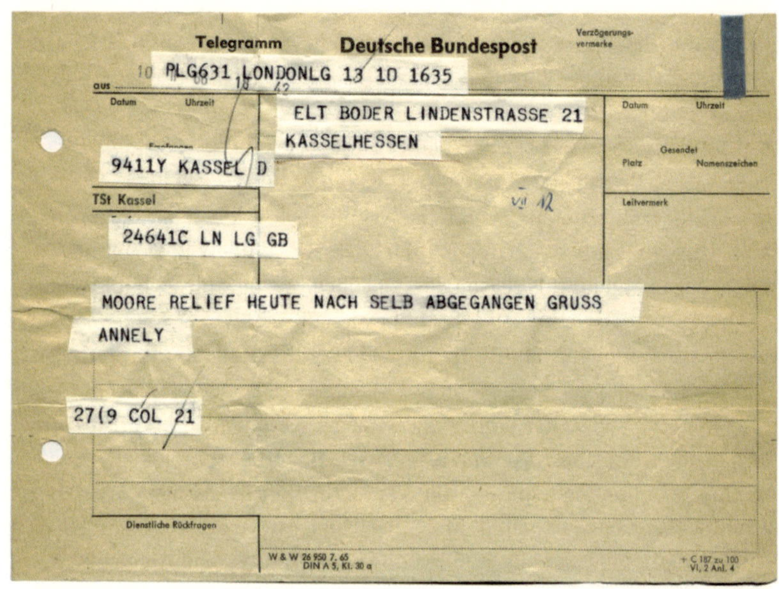

Annely Juda, telegram to Arnold Bode informing him that
Henry Moore's original for one of his reliefs in the Rosenthal
Series has been sent to Selb, November 10, 1966.
Source: Porzellanikon Museum Archive.

[15] Walther Stürmer, 'Bei Rosenthal. Die
Relief-Reihe'. In Wilhelm Siemen [ed.],
*Begegnungen - Zeitgenössische
Porzellanplastik*. Hohemberger an der Eger:
Deutsches Porzellan Museum, 1999, p. 48.

[16] Ibid., p. 51.

[17] Ibid., p. 51.

[18] Almir Mavignier, letter to Arnold Bode,
June 13, 1966, Arnold Bode documenta
archiv estate, 126, fol. 65.

discarded the idea, but only because it would have required a layer of glaze that would have dulled the edges and taken away the delicacy the sculptor wanted for this piece. Instead, he opted to give it a coating of shellac, which he applied himself when the porcelain was cold. For us "porcelainers", it made the hairs on the back of our necks stand on end.'[15]

As for Lucio Fontana, whom Bode admired very much and who had had a major presence at documenta II, he was already very ill when the project began and for this reason did not conceive a new piece, but instead sent four sketches of *Concetti spaziali* he already had to be made up at Rosenthal's studio. Walter Stürmer would later describe the enormous technical difficulties they encountered when materialising Fontana's prototypes, which consisted of '...objects turned or moulded in earthenware, cracked or perforated'.[16] The first tests showed that using moulds to transfer onto the porcelain the fractures and slits on the models did not work, so another solution had to be found. 'In the evening, after everyone had gone, I would take a knife and burin and try to make the holes, slits and cuts in the soft porcelain. Little by little the aesthetics of destroying, cutting and piercing became apparent to me. Each time the results came a little closer to the four Fontana sample objects I had been given.[17] Fontana would eventually choose three of the four objects Stürmer had made, and in 1968 they were produced in editions of 75 copies, each with the titles *Concetto spaziale ovale*, *Concetto spaziale taglio* and *Concetto spaziale cratere*.

The objections or challenges the Relief Series project came up against were not always of a technical nature, however. In several cases, artists expressed doubts as to the true identity of the project, which they thought did not clearly address the disjunction between decoration – applied art – and artistic creation per se. Illustrating this is the reaction to Rosenthal's invitation of Almir Mavignier, a Brazilian artist and designer based in Europe since the 1950s whose painting and prints transited the realms of concrete painting and op art: 'If Mr. Rosenthal could see my posters and catalogues, perhaps he would entrust me with the creation of a new advertising style for his products,' he responded in a letter to Bode. 'But if he considers the dot structures of my work to be merely decorative applications on porcelain, I would have to transform these structures into ornamentation. I try to understand Mr Rosenthal's interest, but I am so obsessed with the use of such structures as a means to an end – namely, to achieve a new optical effect in painting – that their use as ornament alone, that is, as an end only, would mean firstly an interruption of my activity as a painter, and secondly running a risk of kitschification by repeating such structures in industrial use...'[18] When informed by Bode of Mavignier's doubts,

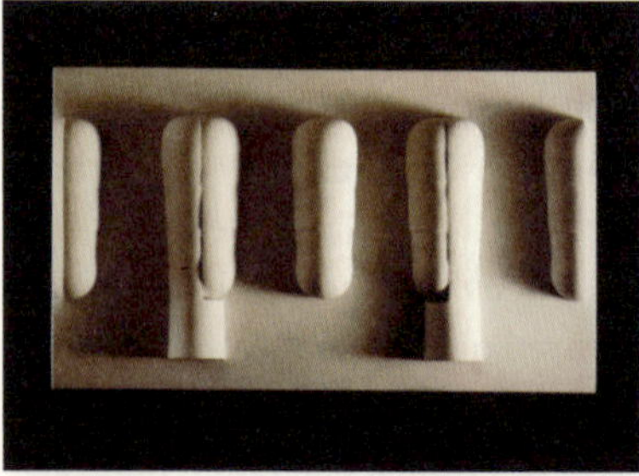

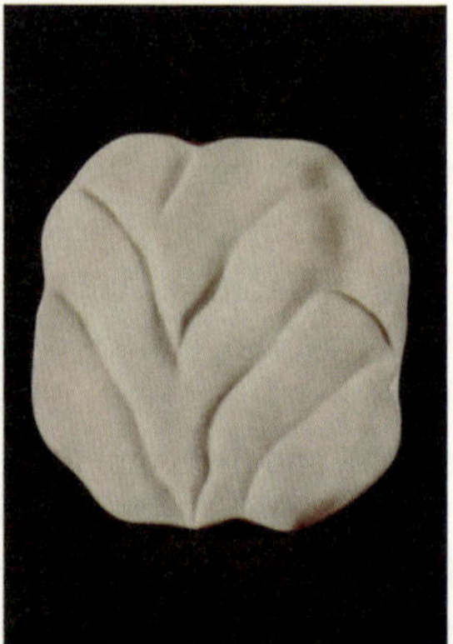

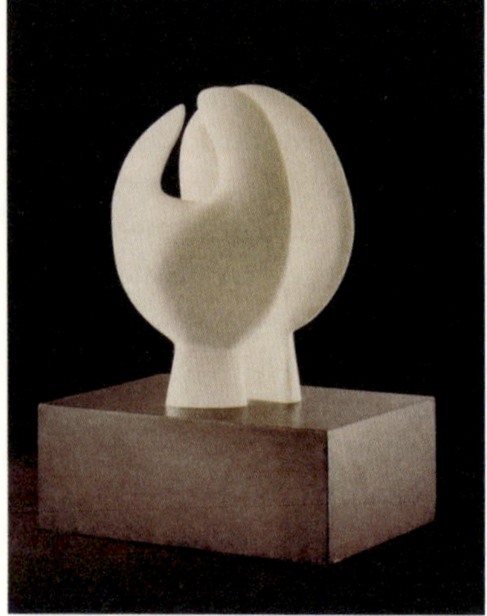

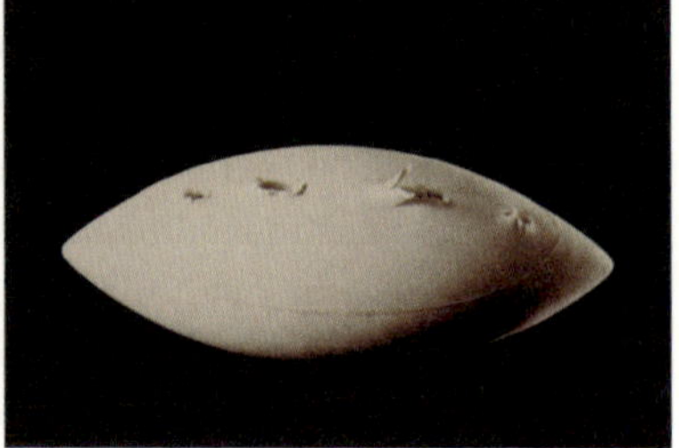

Reliefs by Joannis Avramidis, Emil Cimiotti,
Henry Moore and Lucio Fontana for the
Rosenthal Series, 1968.
Photo: Porzellanikon Museum Archive.

19 Philip Rosenthal, letter to Almir
Mavignier, July 28, 1966, Arnold Bode
documenta archiv estate, 126, fol. 51.

20 The title of *ars porcellana - Die Rosenthal
Relief Reihe* was inspired by *ars multiplicata*,
the title of the exhibition of multiples and
editions held in the same Kunsthalle a few
months earlier, organised by Hein Stünke.
Unfortunately, the choice of *ars porcellana*
played a little etymological trick on the
organisers, as the press was only too quick
to point out: '*ars multiplicata* tripped off
the tongue so delightfully, the Rosenthal
company thought *ars porcellana* would
sound just as natural, beautifully clear and
convincing, and did not think to consult a
dictionary. *Errare humanum est!* The evil
humanist suspicion is confirmed: *porcellana*
in Latin means anything but 'porcelain', as
porcelain had not yet been invented. It is but
the adjective for *porcella* – female pig.' G. Z.,
'ars porcellana?' In *Frankfurter Allgemeine
Zeitung*, no. 213, September 13, 1968.

Rosenthal immediately replied to the painter, assuring him that it was not
an ornamental design he was asking for: 'When I saw your works at the
documenta, I did not imagine that you would now be applying or adapting
such similar decorative motifs to existing forms. That always devalues,
although I think it is a mistake of our times to believe that aesthetic quality
depends on pieces being unique or reproduced only in small numbers. [...]
My idea has long been that decoration can only receive new impetus from
artistic freedom, and that combining verve with formal resolution must also
be possible in our times. For example, one should be able to design large
vases and similar objects according to the Alhambra principle. Not in style,
of course, but in spirit...'[19]

Mavignier eventually accepted the invitation and produced a relief that
would actually be one of the most interesting in the series. The optical effect
he sought in his paintings and serigraphs through complex arrangements
of coloured dots was simplified: the dots were enlarged and transformed
into cones, making them three-dimensional, which brought into play effects
caused by changes in light, shadows, and viewer perspectives.

A substantial part of the Rosenthal Relief Series was presented –
and put on sale – in documenta IV together with the other editions of the
documenta foundation. The reliefs' 'fifteen minutes of fame' did not happen
in Kassel, however, but in an exhibition dedicated to the series that took
place immediately after documenta at the Kölnischer Kunstverein, entitled
ars porcellana - The Rosenthal Relief Series.[20] Curated by Arnold Bode with
the support of Sturmer and the Rosenthal company, which subsidised a
large part of the costs, the exhibition was announced as the first of a series
of public presentations of the project which, Bode said, were forthcoming,
but which in fact never took place.

While it appears that preparations for this exhibition had begun before
documenta IV, there is, strikingly, no mention of the documenta foundation
in Bode's first letter of proposal to the Kunstverein, perhaps – one might
speculate – because the relationship between the foundation (or some of
its members?) and Rosenthal AG were not entirely fluid. In it, Bode was
careful to dispel any misgivings that might arise from the concession of
a public space for the display of products destined for sale and financed
by a private entrepreneur, even if it had been stipulated that 30% of the
revenue from the sales of the reliefs would go to the Kölnischer Kunstverein:
'Rosenthal is only the manufacturer, and his company does not exploit
the reliefs commercially. This is about opening up opportunities for new
sculpture through the use of porcelain, a great material. The reliefs will be
cast in series of 50-100 pieces, numbered and signed like prints. Producing

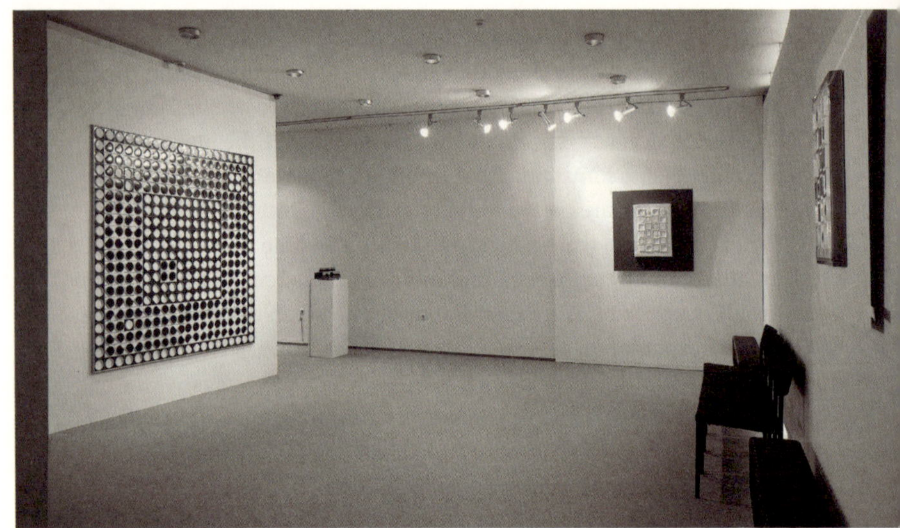

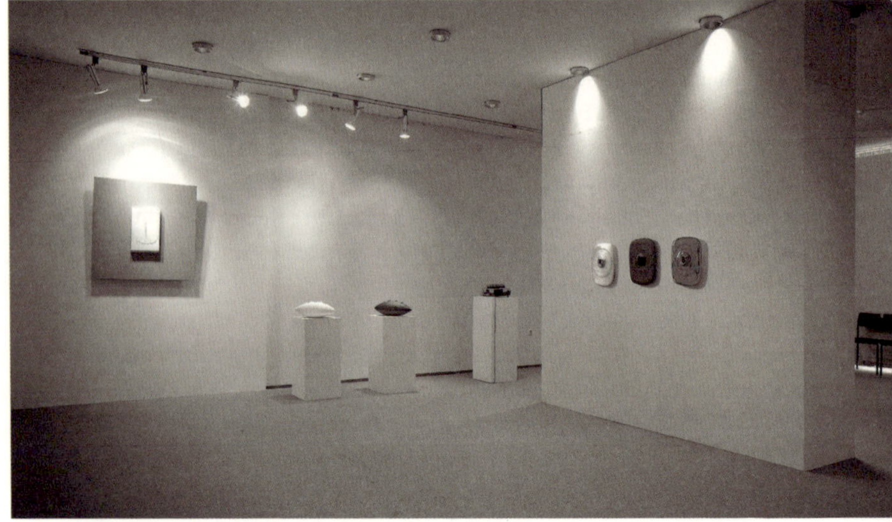

Exhibition view of *ars porcellana*, Kölnischer Kunstverein, 1968.
Photo: Clemens Hartzenbusch.

21 Arnold Bode, letter to Toni Feldenkirchen
    [Director of the Kölnischer Kunstverein],
    December 16, 1967, Historisches Archiv
    der Stadt Köln – HASTK, inventory no. 1968
    [Kölnischer Kunstverein], ACC500-A12.

22 G. Z., op. cit.

objects in series is the in-thing right now. I think that materialisations of
an artwork, like this, without an original, will also be an opportunity for
the artist and for the young collector. Rosenthal wants to use this initiative
to establish contacts with important artists and enhance the image of his
company through its links with art. A small jury (Bode, Dr. von Buttlar and
Dr. Wolters) will prepare the exhibition on behalf of Rosenthal and publish
the catalogue. I myself will design the exhibition and the costs will be borne
by Rosenthal AG. Any accusation that this is a commercial enterprise can be
dismissed. I can talk to the gentlemen on your board of directors personally
if you think it appropriate.'[21]

ars porcellana opened its doors in September 1968, just after the end
of the fourth documenta and just before the second edition of the Cologne
Art Fair was due to open in October of that year. Despite its impeccable
display design, which was of Arnold Bode's customary high standard,
the exhibition was met with scepticism, not because the idea of showing
'works without originals' did not arouse interest but because the quality
of the works did not convince, as the *Frankfurter Allgemeine Zeitung's*
review of the exhibition spelled out: '...Of the twenty-two artists, only two
– Almir Mavignier and Ferdinand Ris – actually bring a new artistic aspect
to porcelain, and they do so only on a modest scale. The majority have
delivered graphic work on porcelain, but then a print is cheaper and an
original better. Vasarely, an artist who is attracting more attention for his
prices than for his quality, is asking an eye-watering DM 12,000 for each of
his porcelain tapestries...'[22]

Partly because of the exhibition's poor reception, Bode's consultancy
work for Rosenthal came to an end with *ars porcellana*, and with it, the
documenta foundation's collaboration with Rosenthal. At the porcelain
company, Bode would be replaced by Eugen Gomringer, who single-
handedly took on the task of inviting new artists to continue the Relief
Series. Salvador Dalí, Friedensreich Hundertwasser, Roy Lichtenstein, Otto
Piene, Eduardo Paolozzi, Nikki de Saint Phalle and Paul Wunderlich are
some of the artists he brought to the project, followed later by Jean Cocteau,
Tom Wesselmann, Ferdinand Krivet, Max Bill and himself, who also
designed a piece for the series.

The experiment that was the collaboration between Arnold Bode,
acting on behalf of the documenta foundation, and the Rosenthal company
is not uninteresting. From Bode's perspective, the collaboration had aimed
to provide a practical answer to some of the questions that the introduction
of industrial manufacturing methods had sparked among artists since
the beginning of the twentieth century. For Rosenthal, the mere prospect

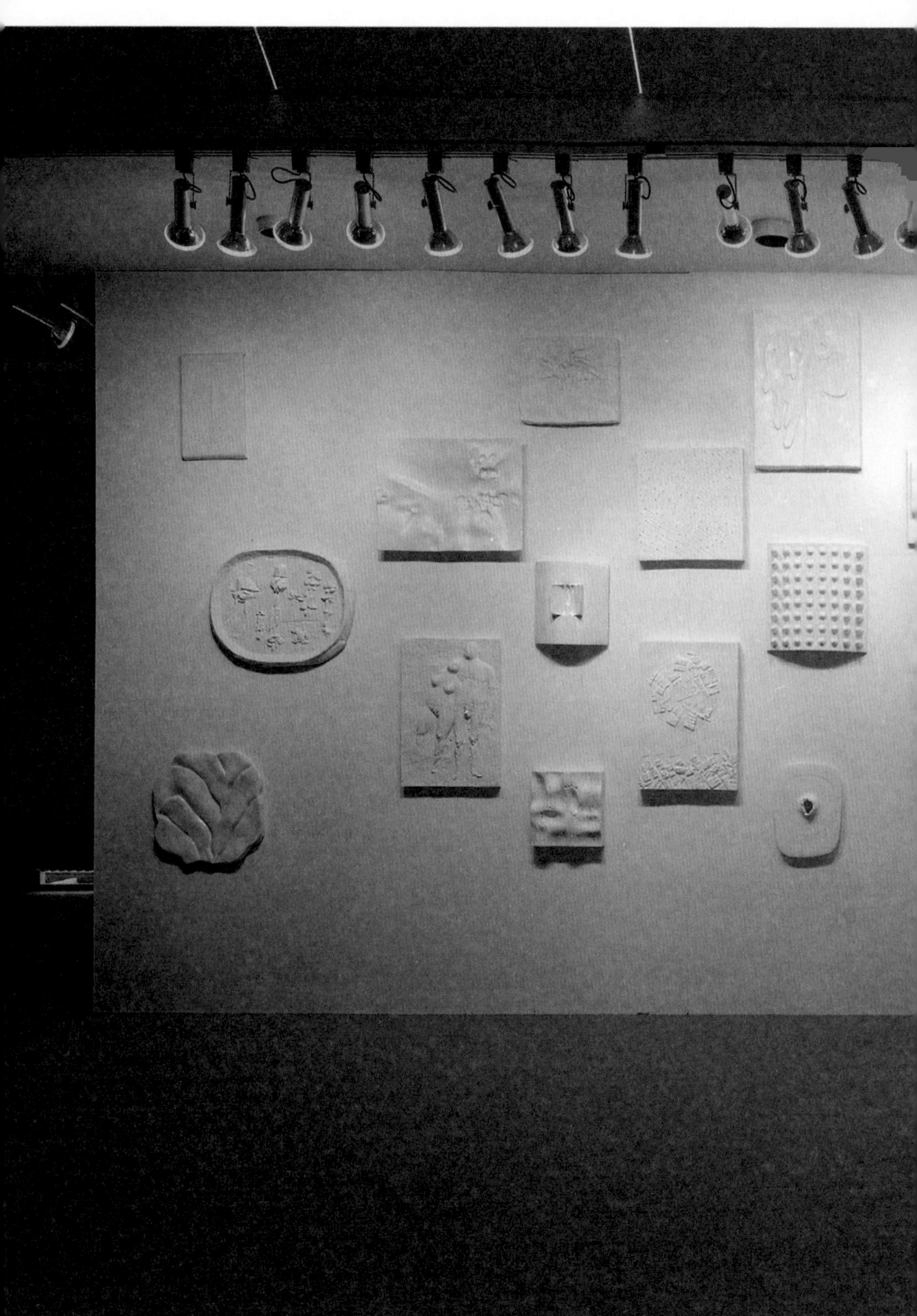

Exhibition view of *ars porcellana*, Kölnischer Kunstverein, 1968.
Photo: Clemens Hartzenbusch.

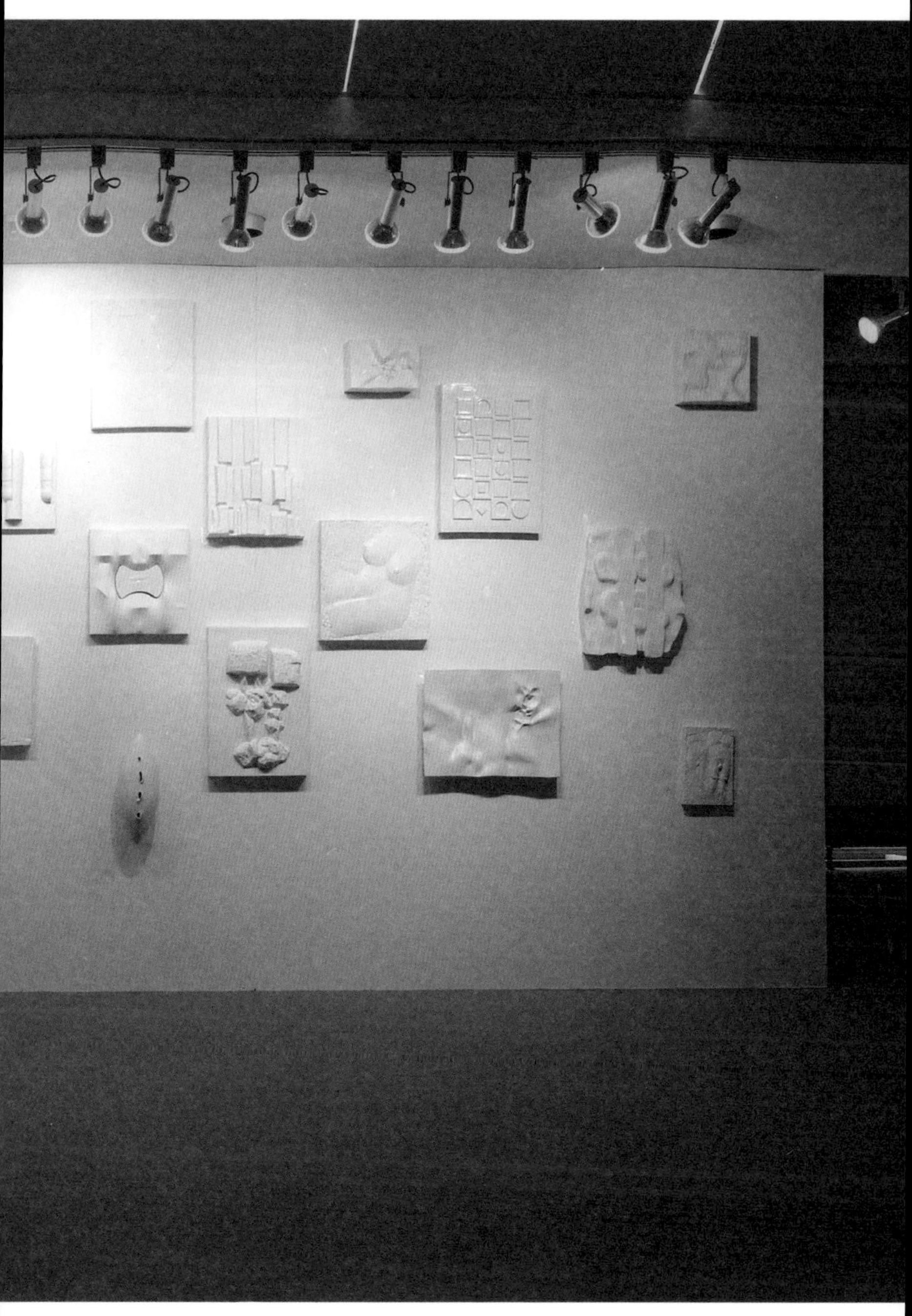

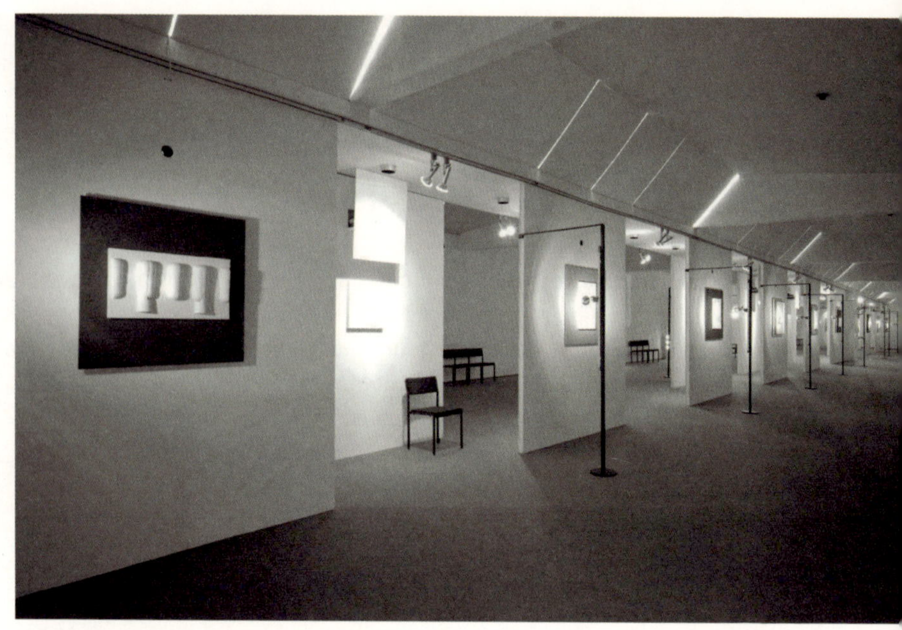

Exhibition view of *ars porcellana*, Kölnischer Kunstverein, 1968.
Photo: Clemens Hartzenbusch.

23 See Dieter Honisch, 'Kunst gebrauchen.
Versuch einer Analyse von Kunst und Design bei
Rosenthal'. In *Die Rosenthal Story*, op. cit. p. 44.

24 Edith Benkhe, *Limitierte Kunstobjekte
in Porzellan, 1968-2003*, doctoral
dissertation, Faculty of Philosophy of
the Rheinische Friedrich-Wilhelms
Universität, Bonn, 2011, pp. 3, 43.

25 Josephine Gabler, 'Rosenthal Relief Reihe,
Reliefkunst in den sechziger Jahren'. In
Edith Behnke and Josephine Gabler (eds.),
ars porcellana - Die Rosenthal Relief Reihe.
Wörlen: Museum Moderner Kunst, 2009, p. 28.

of collaborating with the artists was the appeal, regardless of the artistic result, and as Bode astutely pointed out in his letter to the director of the Kölnischer Kunstverein, the relationship had been good for the company's corporate image. However, the Series, rather than providing answers, raised more questions: Was the aim really to popularise these porcelain pieces as 'autonomous art', or to make a profit? If the intention had been to manufacture art objects for the general public, why were the reliefs produced in relatively limited runs and not mass-produced?[23] The gap between fine art and applied arts continued to exist and undercut the entire project. Art history would not legitimise the artistic value of the porcelain series – whose pieces were quickly engulfed by the course of history and today are barely remembered at all. Besides, porcelain continued to be associated in the collective mind with decoration – *ostentatious* decoration – an association that the porcelain figures of the late Baroque and Rococo periods did not help to dissipate, and Bode and Rosenthal's collaboration did not entirely succeed in overcoming this preconception.[24]

It is therefore debatable whether the two men's mission to promote a 'renaissance' of porcelain as an artistic material achieved its aims. Stigmatised as a decorative material, porcelain failed to arouse the expected interest among either the art public, porcelain enthusiasts, or even artists, as is evidenced by the fact that those artists who took part in the project rarely included the porcelain pieces they had made for Rosenthal among their achievements and assigned them only a rather anecdotal relevance in their careers. In the words of Josephine Gabler, 'for sculpture lovers, porcelain had the same decorative aftertaste as it had for artists, and therefore the objects in the Rosenthal series were rarely considered as sculpture, but rather as handicraft. For those interested in the decorative arts, in turn, the reliefs were too sculptural and not ornamental enough. And no one seemed to associate these art works with the multiples produced by Pop art, i.e. with mass-produced art objects.'[25]

The art market takes off:
ars consumenda

---

[1] Rudolf Zwirner, *Ich wollte immer Gegenwart. Autobiographie*, op. cit., p. 57.

[2] Ibid., p. 68.

The Rosenthal Relief Series experiment was not the success everyone had anticipated in terms of its aesthetic appreciation, and even less commercially. Other kinds of market-oriented experiences within the context of documenta did, however, prove more fruitful, at least for some of the parties concerned. In particular, Hein Stünke and Rudolf Zwirner, the only two gallery owners that had actively participated in the exhibition's first editions, gained invaluable experience in Kassel which would prove crucial to both their careers.

Stünke and Zwirner had known each other since Zwirner was a child, growing up in Braunschweig, where his parents had become acquainted with the Stünkes during Hein's stint at the Hitler Youth Leadership School. In 1955, young Zwirner visited the first documenta and was so impressed that he immediately decided to abandon his law studies and devote himself to art. His family's friendship with Stünke then paved the way for his first internship, which took place at Galerie Der Spiegel. Shortly afterwards, Zwirner moved to Paris to continue his training and it was while he was in France, in December 1958, that he received an offer to join the production team of the second documenta: 'I received a telegram from Hein Stünke asking me to come to Cologne because Arnold Bode wanted to meet me at his gallery the next day or day after for a job interview. The two men had been friends since the first documenta. For documenta II, Stünke was on the advisory board and had recommended me for the post of general secretary.'[1]

After an interview with Bode in Cologne and another with Herbert von Buttlar in Hamburg, Zwirner joined a team that was anything but large, as he recalled years later: the production of the second documenta was to fall entirely on him, supported only by a secretary and an assistant. Once again, however, despite the meagre team structure and the very short time available for preparations, the exhibition was duly ready in June, and the response from the media as well as visitor figures not only matched but exceeded those of the previous edition.

documenta II's success with the public manifested itself in many different ways, one of which, as already mentioned, was the public's enthusiastic response to the improvised idea of offering prints for sale next to the graphic art exhibition. To help them run the stall, the Stünkes had hired a student called Ursula Reppin, who would later become Zwirner's first wife. Zwirner recalled that 'Ursula not only issued the invoices, she also noted down the customers' addresses. When we opened my gallery in Essen the following year, that impressive address file was a good resource for us'.[2] Zwirner's contract with documenta came to an end in November 1959, but in October he had already begun to look for a location in Essen to open a space of his own as soon as his collaboration in Kassel was over. The professional experience gained in those early formative years had confirmed to Zwirner that his interest in contemporary art was genuine and that his role in the art world would be that of a gallery owner.

Hein Stünke, for his part, felt that the unexpected success of the sales had had a significant pedagogical impact on both himself and Zwirner: 'I had hired Ursula,[3] Zwirner's wife, to run my sales stand, and she witnessed with us the furore unleashed by graphic art. For Zwirner and me it was an eye-opener: we had to find a way of introducing people directly to art, like in antiques fairs: you should be able to take things in your hands and look at them without feeling pressured. You didn't *have to* buy, but you *could* buy; and the aim was, of course, to sell!'[4]

That impact would have several consequences. Firstly, it convinced the documenta organisers, once and for all, of the benefits of creating an entity that could publish and distribute its own editions (rather than simply market those of others), paving the way for the creation of the documenta foundation in 1964. Secondly – though perhaps in a way that was not entirely transparent – the sale of graphic work would provide the Zwirners with a source of information about buyers, their addresses and their tastes which proved helpful when they set up their own gallery a few months later. And, more importantly, both Stünke and Zwirner began to realise just how much of an appetite there was among the public for buying works of art, and how much that curiosity could be stimulated by an environment like documenta: a well-attended public event, where one could come into close contact with the works and where the offer was wide and varied. This intuition would be shared even by Bode himself, who, as Zwirner recalled, suggested they involve their art galleries in the next documenta.[5] Although tempted by the chance to milk documenta's public appeal to promote their own private ventures, Zwirner and Stünke came to the decision that rather than partnering with documenta they would set up their own project in Cologne, the city where Galerie Der Spiegel was based and to which Zwirner would presently relocate his business.

---

[3] Ursula Reppin recalls the same episode in an interview. [http://audioarchivkunst.de/zeitzeugen/ursula-reppin/, retrieved in September 2021].

---

[4] Birgit Maria Sturm, op. cit., p. 21.

[5] Julia Voss, 'Interview mit Rudolf Zwirner'. In Raphael Gross et al. [eds.], op. cit., p. 264.

---

[6] Rudolf Zwirner, *Ich wollte immer Gegenwart. Autobiographie*, op. cit., p. 82.

The idea of 'doing something in Cologne' still had to mature, however, and that would take time. In 1959, Zwirner had founded his gallery in Essen, starting a close collaboration with the Stünke family whose framing and graphic art business he had relied on in those early days, thanks to the commissions he received each time he redirected services to Galerie Der Spiegel.[6] Then, in 1962, Galerie Zwirner had moved to Cologne, where a local scene with a strong interest in contemporary art practices and a significant, albeit small, group of collectors contributed to an improvement in sales. In 1964, documenta III took place, the documenta foundation was publicly launched, and its editions and the porcelain pieces of the Rosenthal Relief Series were put on sale. Once again, the success of the foundation's sales during the exhibition in Kassel exceeded all expectations.

Not long after, in 1966, Zwirner and Stünke felt that the time had come to take the plunge. Both had observed several phenomena occur in recent years that supported their decision: not only had the number of contemporary art galleries increased in the Federal Republic, but these had ceased to be merely places of commercial exchange and had become 'art spaces' in their own right – small, perhaps, but with a far from negligible impact. Simultaneously, all over the country, interest in multiples and graphic art had been growing, which consequently revitalised a segment of the market that had previously shied away from buying. On the other hand, Pop art, the art trend *du jour*, was being marketed by foreign galleries, and the few German galleries that had taken a chance with it felt that their efforts to popularise it were not paying off. Everything seemed to indicate that the time was ripe. After garnering support from their professional colleagues, Zwirner and Stünke approached Kurt Hackenberg, head of culture at Cologne's City Council, with a proposal to organise an art fair in the city dedicated exclusively to contemporary art.

Hackenberg received the idea positively, but explained that they first needed to constitute an official entity that would allow them to negotiate with the institutions on their behalf, or on behalf of a group of gallery owners.

In addition to Zwirner and Stünke, sixteen other galleries expressed a commitment to the initiative: Aenne Abels, Cologne; Rudolf Springer and René Block, Berlin; Tobies & Silex Gallery, Cologne; Otto Stangl, Otto van der Loo and Raimund Thomas, Munich; Hans Mayer and Wilfried Reckermann, Esslingen; Hans-Jürgen Müller, Stuttgart; Dieter Brusberg from Hanover, Rolf Ricke from Kassel, Hans Neuendorf from Hamburg, the Appel und Fertsch gallery in Frankfurt and the Schmela and Gunar galleries

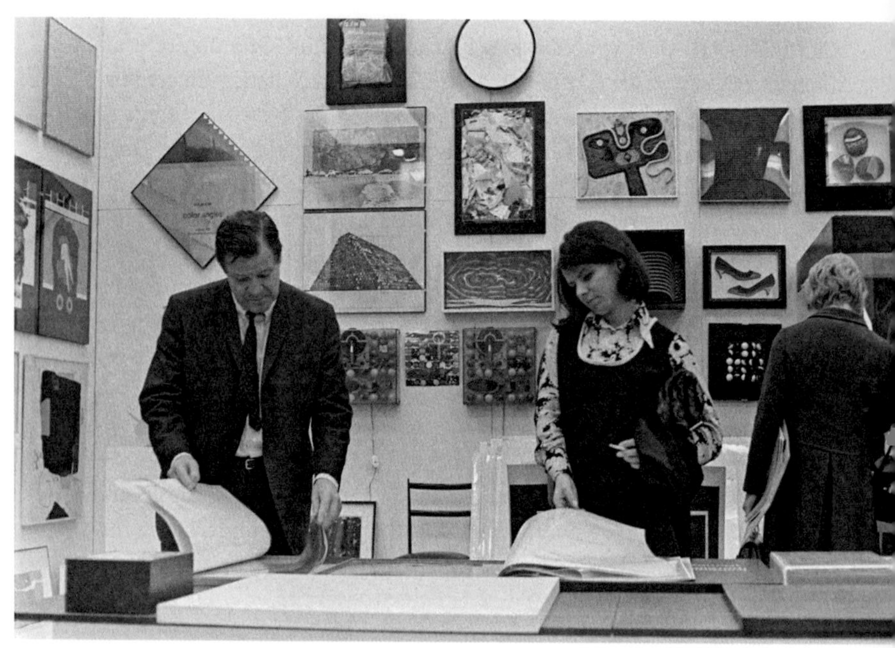

Hein Stünke in his stand at the second
edition of the Cologne Art Fair, 1968.
Photo: Angelika Platen.

[7] Katharina Schmidt, op. cit.

[8] The *Kölner Progressive,* which included the
photographer August Sander and the painters
Franz Wilhelm Seiwert and Heinrich Hoerle,
who shared an interest in documenting
the social structures of their time.

[9] For details of the history of the Cologne
Art Fair, see Zentralarchiv für Deutsche
und Internationale Kunstmarktforschung
– ZADIK [ed.], op. cit.

[10] Günter Herzog, 'Kunstmarkt
Köln 67', in ibid., p. 26.

in Düsseldorf.[7] Following Hackenberg's advice, in July 1966 they officially founded the Association of Progressive German Art Galleries, chaired by Hein Stünke and with Rudolf Zwirner as secretary.

It might seem that the word 'progressive' in the association's name was a nod to the self-styled 'Cologne Progressives', a group of artists which had been active in the city during the 1920s,[8] or that it signalled certain political attitudes, but this was not the case. In fact, the adjective was intended to distinguish the members of the association, who embraced contemporary artistic practices, from other German dealers and gallery owners (which were the majority), whose interests and activities focused on more classical periods of art.

Once officially founded, the Association was able to dodge the hurdles arising from the plan to organise a commercial and clearly profit-oriented activity in a public space thanks to Hackenberg's political power in the City Council. The groundwork advanced swiftly, and soon the City Council announced that one of its official spaces, the Gürzenich, would house the event.

And so, from September 13 to 17, 1967, the Gürzenich accommodated the first edition of the Cologne Art Fair in which the eighteen galleries forming the Association took part. The organisers had expected visitor numbers to be in the region of two thousand, but over the five days the fair was open, some fifteen thousand people came to see it, making purchases that totalled over one million marks.[9] It was a resounding success, as the press did not fail to echo both in Germany and internationally. It was also the beginning of a project that has continued to this day, whose real achievement would take some time to fully recognise. Only with the perspective of history has it become clear that the Cologne Art Fair was the torchbearer that led the way for Art Basel, Frieze, Artissima, FIAC, ARCO and so many other contemporary international fairs, provoking a radical paradigm change in the art market, which would cease to be as elitist as it was discreet to become uncomplicated, extroverted, massive... and increasingly powerful.

In accounting for this success, it has been suggested that 'what was revolutionary [...] was the experience of being able to buy things that previously could only have been contemplated in exhibitions and museums'.[10] However, this statement does not entirely reflect the reality, as the exhibited art works *were already* on sale in certain contexts, such as the Kunstvereine, some thematic exhibitions and, of course, documenta, as we have seen. The possibility of purchasing cannot, by itself, explain Cologne Art Fair's tremendous success – there must have been other factors.

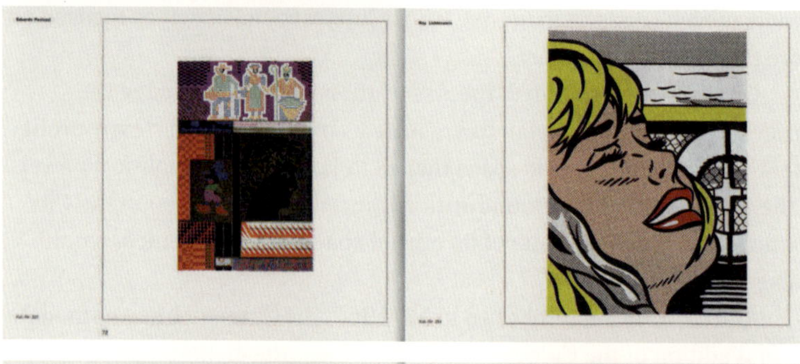
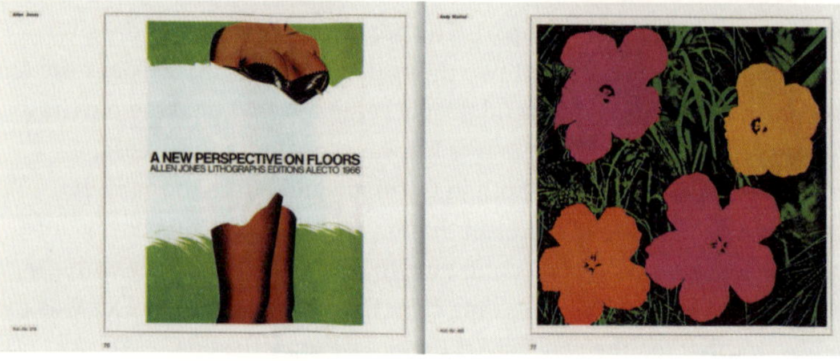

ars multiplicata exhibition catalogue,
Kölnischer Kunstverein, 1968.

[11] Hein Stünke quoted in Heiner Stachelhaus, 'Köln wird zum Kunsthandelszentrum'. In *Ruhr Nachrichten*, January 27, 1967.

[12] Rolf-Gunter Dienst, op. cit., p. 9.

[13] Ibid., p. 9.

[14] Press release for the dissemination of *ars multiplicata*, Historisches Archiv der Stadt Köln – HASTK, inventory no. 1968 [Kölnischer Kunstverein], ACC500-A12.

Some of these may have been specific to art: for example, the art world's aspiration to become part of mass culture, the association between collecting and social status that appealed to so many, or Cologne's desire to have a thriving local contemporary art scene. Other factors probably had to do with new social habits more broadly, such as the exponential growth of consumption or even the reconfiguration of physical retail environments that had begun after the Second World War, when models such as the supermarket, which offered all kinds of products under one roof, had rapidly caught on. Indeed, Stünke had seemed particularly sensitive to the importance of the physical setting of sales: 'The closer you are to each other, the better business goes for everyone,' he is quoted as saying a few months before the fair;[11] and, shortly afterwards: 'Look at the difference between a fair and, say, the documenta. The public at an art fair is more lively. They don't just stand in front of the works and look at them, they pick things up if they wish, hold the prints in their hands or tinker with the objects. That's the advantage of fairs and it's what makes them so attractive.'[12]

Analysing the reasons for the sudden success of print sales in the 1960s falls beyond the scope of this book, but it is clear that the line between spaces for the commercial exchange of artwork and institutional exhibition contexts was very blurred in those years and would remain so for quite some time. Just how porous the line was is demonstrated by the exhibition that the Association of Progressive German Art Galleries installed in the Kunstverein in Cologne to coincide with their art fair. For this exhibition, which ran for two months, each of the galleries participating in the fair was allowed to present work by one or two artists. The works were for sale (of course!) and the prices, which included the mandatory commission for the Kunstverein, were clearly visible in the exhibition spaces. Rudolf Zwirner would later reproach himself for not having produced a more conceptually rigorous exhibition, that is, one curated by an expert.[13] But the fact is, the formula chosen for this show mirrored a way of understanding the symbiosis between exhibition and art commerce that was unexceptional at the time.

Another example of this symbiosis was *ars multiplicata*, an exhibition Hein Stünke organised at the Kunstverein a few months after the Cologne Art Fair, which ran along similar lines. 'The exhibition programme includes celebrated post-1945 works by the greats of French modernism as well as prints from the various currents of 1950s European art. The focus, however, will be on the younger generation of mostly American artists, i.e. on Pop art and Op art. Among the many contributions to the exhibition, the Italian one will be especially remarkable.'[14] Thus read the rather vague description of the exhibition used in the press release sent out to announce *ars multiplicata. Serial Art since 1945*,[15] held at the Kölnischer Kunstverein from January to April 1968. A lavishly illustrated catalogue[16] was brought out for the occasion. In the prologue, it was revealed that not only had the project been Hein Stünke's idea, but that he had participated in the selection of works and lent a significant number of the pieces.[17] It also mentioned that anyone interested in purchasing any of the works on display in *ars multiplicata* should not hesitate to contact the Kunsthalle's secretariat.

Surprisingly, some of the writers that featured in the catalogue expressed strong misgivings about the concept of serial art – the very basis of the exhibition. Art historian Gerd von der Osten, director of the Wallraf-Richartz Museum in Cologne, pointed to the instant gratification of modern consumer needs as one of the dangers facing the multiple: 'It is true that reproduction and multiplication have a lot to do with consumerism. In this sense, the path of art leads to the vastness of the people (in their potential as owners of art). As Hermann Schnitzler said, *ars multiplicata* is also *ars consumenda*. Given the pull of these art products, the curator in us, who wishes to preserve, hopes that what glitters today will not one day become *ars consumpta*: worn-out, consumed art. It is precisely the mass-produced that is easily the most ephemeral.'[18] In turn, Erhart Kästner, former director of the Herzog August Bibliothek in Wolfenbüttel for almost twenty years, expressed concerns about the possible threat of alienation concealed in the exercise of multiplication, which he believed was linked to the contemporary desire to forsake individuality and blend in with a mass of consumers, all with identical references and opinions: 'One cannot understand the

[15] *ars multiplicata. Vervielfältigte Kunst seit 1945*, exhibition from January 12 to April 15, 1968. Organised by the Wallraf-Richartz-Museum in the Kunsthalle Köln. At the time, in Cologne the Kunsthalle and the Kunstverein were located in the same place.

[16] *ars multiplicata: Vervielfältigte Kunst seit 1945*. Cologne: Kölnischer Kunstverein, 1968.

[17] Though not mentioned in the foreword, the preparatory documentation reveals that Galerie Der Spiegel undertook part of the installation work, invoicing the Kunstverein for more than DM 30,000. See Cologne Historical Archives [HASTK], inventory 1386 [Kölnischer Kunstverein], ACC500-A12.

[18] Gert von den Osten, 'Original / Reproduktion / Multiplikation'. In *ars multiplicata: Vervielfältigte Kunst seit 1945*, op. cit., p. 17.

[19] Erhart Kästner, 'X mal Buch', in *ars multiplicata: Vervielfältigte Kunst seit 1945*, op. cit., p. 18.

[20] Hein Stünke, 'Graphik und Objekte: Einige Daten zu ihrer Geschichte von 1945 bis heute', in *ars multiplicata: Vervielfältigte Kunst seit 1945*, op. cit. pp. 46-53.

[21] Peter M. Bode, 'Das Kunstwerk im Zeitalter seiner technischen Multiplizierbarkeit. Zur Ausstellung *ars multiplicata* in der Kunsthalle Köln'. In *Kölner Stadt-Anzeiger*, January 25, 1968.

attraction of seriality without admitting that it has become not only the fate, but the individual's yearning to be a mass-produced item, a multiple copy: brand-loyal, easily exchanged, manageable, capable only of a suspicious pseudo-existence when the same catchphrases drip into millions of ears. Who would have thought this would be the epitome of happiness? Well, it is. The happiness of casting off the ballast that has made life so difficult for so many thousands of years: one's own person, one's own conscience, one's own destiny, one's own opinion, one's own life and happiness. How pleasant to be part of a mass, to be a multiple. Just a piece with a hole punch.'[19] Kästner went on to trace a more dispassionate review of the history of artists' books, taking his beloved *livres de peintres* as a point of reference, but the beginning of his essay nevertheless leaves a bitter aftertaste of the alienation and depersonalisation serial art seemed to stir in him (which, who knows, perhaps came from personal recollections of his own pre-war political affinities).

Hein Stünke's contribution to the catalogue,[20] on the other hand, was a chronology of what he considered to be the milestones of the history of the multiple, where he gave more importance to folders of prints and other graphic works than to the actual editions of multiple objects. His selection of artists holds no surprises: the School of Paris, the American Abstract Expressionist and Pop painters, besides some other artists, mostly German, who almost invariably had a commercial or professional link with Galerie Der Spiegel. What stands out the most in Stünke's account from today's perspective is the mention of FluxKit, which had been published by George Maciunas in New York in 1963, and of some of Dieter Roth's early books. This mention was inspiring insofar as it represented an opening up to the experimental practices that were beginning to pepper artists' publications, but the interest would never materialise, either on the part of Galerie Der Spiegel or on the part of the documenta foundation where Stünke played a leading role.

Press cuttings kept in archives indicate that public reaction to *ars multiplicata* was highly critical: it escaped no one's notice that what was presented as an ambitious overview of the contemporary multiple was, in reality, little more than the umpteenth exhibition of prints seasoned with a merely symbolic number of genuine multiples. Peter M. Bode rightly objected that 'The title of this exhibition raises expectations that are not fulfilled. No one goes to Cologne just to see an extensive display of arbitrary and unrepresentative graphic works';[21] while Klaus Honnef, in his review, calculated that 'Of the approximately seven hundred objects presented, only seventy are from the field of multiple art.' As if that were not enough,

Honnef added, the few multiples on view at the exhibition were 'mostly objects from the MAT Edition, published by Galerie Der Spiegel in Cologne. (Spiegel's owner, Heinz Stühnke [sic], is on the advisory board of the exhibition *ars multiplicata* and has contributed a history of "multiplicative art from 1945 onwards" to the impressive catalogue).'[22]

The sparks of a conflict that was becoming increasingly difficult to conceal were beginning to fly into the public sphere. And it was not only in the press where the unease caused by the omnipresence of Galerie Der Spiegel and its owner in the most varied cultural initiatives funded by the State was beginning to surface. Artists also began to complain publicly.

Shortly after the opening of *ars multiplicata*, for instance, Wolf Vostell, a member of the Fluxus movement – scarcely represented at the exhibition – asked in his 'First Manifesto to elucidate authoritarian tendencies in Cologne's public cultural institutions': 'This exhibition creates misunderstandings! Why did the management of the Kunsthalle [where the Kunstverein was housed] rely only on the advice of one gallery and publishing house (Galerie Der Spiegel), represented by Hein Stünke on the advisory board? Is it not an act of frivolity not to consult other renowned galleries and publishing houses?'[23]

Barely two months later, the controversy would spread to the documenta foundation. In April, Rudolf Zwirner, who, interestingly, had founded the Association of Progressive German Art Galleries together with Hein Stünke, signed a letter complaining about the damage that the documenta foundation's sales policy was causing galleries: 'Although many galleries have campaigned for years to get these artists recognised, there are no plans to grant them the usual reseller discount on purchases from the

22 Klaus Honnef, 'Kunsthistorische Missverständnisse. Kölner Ausstellung *ars multiplicata* viel unzulänglich aus'. In *Aachener Nachrichten* - 'Das Feuilleton', January 27, 1968, p. 4.

23 Reprinted in Klaus Gereon Beuckers, Hans-Edwin Friedrich and Sven Hanuschek (eds.), *Wolf Vostell: Dé-coll/age als Manifest, Manifest als Dé-coll/age. Manifeste, Aktionsvorträge, Essays.* Munich: edition text + kritik - Richard Boorberg Verlag, 2014, pp. 84-87. Vostell's second 'Manifesto' was directed against the 'authoritarian tendencies in the state cultural institutions of the Federal Republic'

and in particular against documenta, because of the lack of representation of the Fluxus movement in documenta IV.

24 Rudolf Zwirner, letter on behalf of the Association of German Progressive Art Galleries to Hein Stünke, April 5, 1968, documenta archiv, AA, d04, 31, fol. 86. On the 26th of the same month, a copy of the letter is attached to the agenda of a meeting of the Board of Trustees of documenta foundation for discussion.

25 Willi Bongard, 'Was kostet die Documenta? Eine Selbsthilfereaktion stösst auf Kritik'. In *Die Zeit*, April 17, 1968.

documenta foundation editions. This will prevent the editions from being sold through the galleries. We consider this development to be detrimental to contemporary art galleries, since [the documenta foundation], being a non-profit institution, will be exempt from taxation. We therefore ask you to do everything in your power to enable galleries to trade in the documenta foundation's editions.'[24] Although the letter was an internal memo, tensions quickly spilled over into the press and a few days later Willi Bongard wrote a column in *Die Zeit* energetically defending the foundation's actions and accusing galleries of shooting themselves in the foot by obstructing the work of a non-profit organisation. It is 'downright grotesque', lamented Bongard, 'that resistance is coming precisely from these gallery owners, i.e. from the ranks of the Association of Progressive German Art Galleries, which have organised the Cologne Art Fair. After all, if there is anyone to whom documenta directly or indirectly brings economic benefits it is precisely these galleries, most of whose artists are exhibited and admired in Kassel. For there can be no doubt that participation in documenta brings a great gain in prestige, which sooner or later pays off in hard cash.'[25]

On April 29, barely three days after the foundation's trustees meeting at which this letter was discussed, Christoph Vowinckel, then secretary of the documenta foundation, wrote back to the Association countering their arguments. Vowinckel began by pointing out that the foundation had the fiscal status of a non-profit organisation and that, moreover, its members received no fees (with the exception of its managing director, Andreas Vowinckel). He went on to say that the foundation made decisions about each edition in close contact with artists and galleries and rewarded the former for their generosity by giving them a significant part of the print run of each edition, the production of which was entirely subsidised by the foundation's budget. Furthermore, the foundation did not choose pieces on the basis of commercial profitability, as decisions regarding which pieces were to be published rested exclusively with the artists. And it was pointed out that, of course, the entire print run of each edition was never sold. At the recent meeting of the foundation's Board of Trustees, Vowinckel continued, the proposal to offer gallery owners a special discount to compensate them for the resale of the editions has been discussed in detail and discarded because the foundation was non-profit and because the ratio between costs and income was already too tight for the foundation. The foundation, therefore, proposed that interested gallery owners should approach artists to buy their share of each edition and offered to facilitate their contacts.

Finally, Vowinckel's letter addressed the charges levelled against Stünke: 'With regard to the criticism directed against certain members of the Board of Trustees, accusing them of a conflict of interests, I can assure you, having been personally convinced of this, that in no case does a member of the Board of Trustees enjoy indirect advantages, for example by awarding printing or similar commissions to companies close to himself. As far as the distribution of editions is concerned, the foundation's statutes stipulate that the Board of Trustees cannot claim any special rights in this respect. [...] You yourselves know that each new documenta has helped to expand the circle of buyers of modern art considerably. This documenta IV will also give the German art market a substantial and enduring boost. In view of this, it should be in your interest to actively support the efforts of the documenta foundation. I would ask you to refrain from raising any further objections to the work of the foundation, and to actively support the execution of the agreed plans.'[26]

In May, the art critic Georg Jappe covered the controversy in an article[27] in which he identified the three main reasons for the galleries' complaints: firstly, they considered that the documenta foundation was taking advantage of artists by asking them to 'finance' the very same political authorities that should be providing support to documenta: 'If the artist is famous, he brings millions in kind to the region of Hesse for months at a time. If the region, which spends millions on conventional operas, cannot and will not support an exhibition that only takes place every four years and has far more visitors than an opera in the same period, then documenta will explode and the consequences of this stepmotherly valuation of art will be laid bare for all to see.' The galleries' second concern was the unfair competition posed by the documenta foundation, whose expected turnover for 1968 was one third of the total annual retail expenditure on graphic works in the entire country, which would leave many galleries without enough customers to survive. 'The third concern', Jappe concluded, 'lies with the person of Hein Stünke', who 'has gathered in one hand both German and international clients of graphic art, who must also be provided for beyond documenta, once the exhibition is over'. For Jappe, the origin of the crisis essentially lay in the transition that the commercial and cultural structures in art

26 Andreas Vowinckel, letter on behalf of
the documenta foundation to André
Emmerich, Cologne, March 6, 1968,
Zentralarchiv für Deutsche und Internationale
Kunstmarktforschung – ZADIK, A1, IV, 002.

27 Georg Jappe, 'Im Hintergrund der
Documenta. Gericht der Künstler und

Boykott der Kunsthändler'. In *Frankfurter
Allgemeine Zeitung*, May 13, 1968,
documenta archiv, AA, d04, 3.

28 Ibid.

were undergoing. 'The real cause of the crisis is that documenta carries on acting like an untouchable institution at a time when institutions are being dismantled. Artists and art dealers are "coming of age". They no longer feel respect for a hypothetically good cause and will only be convinced by a cause that is inherently good.'[28]

The beginning of the end

1 Court of Audit of the State of Hessen. Audit
of the use of federal and state subsidies
granted for the realisation of the documenta
II art exhibition. Darmstadt, 'Conclusion and
execution of contracts' [item 6c], September
4, 1961, p. 10, documenta archiv, AA, d02, 51.

The social and political dissatisfaction that had been spreading across the Western world for some time came to a head in the spring of 1968 in the form of revolts across Europe, triggering a crisis in which institutional authority – of which cultural institutions were a part – was seriously challenged. It was in this climate of widespread convulsion that the collision of private commercial gain and institutional artistic function at the core of documenta hit the media and the wider public.

In Hein Stünke's particular case, the problem that was now coming to light had been detected long before – practically at the same time that the web of interests between art and commerce first began to form as a consequence of his role in documenta as both provider of professional services and member of the organising team. Indeed, ever since the second edition of documenta, his double 'identity' as a provider of storage, transport, framing and installation services *and also* as a member of the curatorial team had been prompting internal complaints. Already in 1961, the Hessian State Court of Auditors had found irregularities in documenta II's allocation of federal and regional subsidies: 'Commission awarded to the company of Hein Stünke, Cologne (installation of graphic work). Here too, it appears from the documents examined that no other local firm was asked to tender for the commission [...] Moreover, it is remarkable that neither Stünke's nor any other firm in Kassel was asked to submit a quotation, and that the representative of the firm in receipt of the commission was Hein Stünke, who is also a member of the committee in charge of selecting graphic artwork. Presumably, Mr. Stünke abstained from voting on the award of the contract insofar as he was party to the assignment.'[1]

As if this were not enough, the continuous toing and froing of relations between documenta and Galerie Der Spiegel that the documenta foundation facilitated were proliferating to such an extent that it was becoming almost impossible to disentangle them, even for the parties involved. The gallery had been taking on an increasingly large share of the production of the documenta foundation's prints and multiples, while simultaneously releasing its own editions by the very same artists, who, in turn, had invariably been previously selected to exhibit in Kassel. Just how entangled this web was is illustrated in the letter sent by Andreas Vowinckel, himself a little disoriented, to the André Emmerich Gallery in New York in 1968, in connection with various commissions under way for the American painter Kenneth Noland:

'Dear Mr Emmerich,

Mrs Stünke, who was in your gallery in January, has handed me a sample of Noland's painting, *Open End 1967* – probably a motif for our edition of prints for the documenta foundation.

I am a little confused, however, since I have received a letter from Mrs Noland telling me that Kenneth Noland has sent you a sample of a painting that he intends to lend to documenta which he would like to make a colour silkscreen reproduction of.

But *Open End 1967* is not a painting that is going to feature in documenta. I believe the sample is intended for the edition that Galerie Der Spiegel in Cologne is preparing. Would you please confirm if I am right or not in my assumptions?

Since the schedule is now very tight, we have begun production using the *Open End* sample, and we would like to ask you for a colour proof of the painting to determine the exact chromatic values.

Moreover, I would be very grateful if you would send us the other sample that Noland originally intended for the documenta foundation, with its colour proof too...'[2]

Finding himself in the eye of the storm yet conscious that his influence in documenta was growing by the day, Hein Stünke did his best to keep a low profile. Ironically, he was reaching the same point as his much-admired Paul Cassirer, the art dealer who in 1901 had had to step down as director of the Berlin Secession annual exhibition because of a similar conflict of interest;[3] but at least for now, Stünke's colleagues at documenta were choosing to look the other way. In the weeks prior to the inauguration of documenta IV, Jean Leering, a member of the working committee for the selection of paintings, pointed out in an internal report

[2] Andreas Vowinckel, letter to André Emmerich, op. cit.

[3] See Regina Schmidt, op. cit.

[4] Internal report by Jean Leering, n.d. (1968). Zentralarchiv für Deutsche und Internationale Kunstmarktforschung – ZADIK, A1, IV, 004.

[5] Birgit Maria Sturm, op. cit., p. 33.

[6] Edward Rathke, 'Ring frei in Kassel'. In *Artis*, no. 2, February 1968, pp. 10-13.

on the status of the editions that the documenta foundation was preparing, that 'As the matrices are not being sent to Kassel but to Cologne, the mistaken belief has spread that the editions are to be produced in Galerie Der Spiegel or its workshop, and all manner of false rumours are circulating, fuelled by the letter sent by the Association of German Art Galleries (which I have not seen).'[4]

For his part, Stünke was unlikely to have been too fazed by the tensions his privileged position ignited. In an interview given years later, he conceded that his considerable influence, which was increasingly the object of criticism, was due to his proximity to artists: 'Yes, power comes from there too, from the influence they sometimes have. Art dealers and gallery owners are, in a sense, "extended artists". They have exclusive access; they go into studios and workshops. Ask an art historian or a museologist if they have ever been inside an artist's studio!'[5]

Indeed, Stünke was not the only one, by any means, to be caught in this complex web of interpersonal and interprofessional relations that had woven itself around documenta. In February 1968, the director of the Frankfurter Kunstverein, Ewald Rathke, complained bitterly about the endogamic nature of documenta Board members and pointed the finger at Hein Stünke, although not solely at him: '…[After all] who could possibly suspect anything underhand? Willi Bongard, for example, is a member of documenta's Press and Information committee. In his recently published book, *Kunst und Kommerz*, he describes Hein Stünke, owner of Galerie Der Spiegel in Cologne, as one of the most progressive art gallerists in Europe, as someone who defends an innovative and revolutionary conception of artwork and the art market. In turn, Hein Stünke accepts an invitation by Professor Herbert von Buttlar, director of the Hamburg School [of Fine Arts], to give the semester's inaugural talk; Von Buttlar is also chairman of the documenta organising committee and oversees *Ambiente* and the Press and Information working group. [Almir] Mavignier teaches at the Hamburg School of Fine Arts, and Hein Stünke, a member of the documenta Board, reproduces and sells this artist's graphic work through his gallery. Only the ill-intentioned would find anything amiss in such a chain of relationships…'[6]

What did artists think of all this? Among them too, signs of disconformity and discontent had begun to show. Wolf Vostell was among the first to speak out, with his manifestos protesting at the absence of Fluxus representation in documenta IV and in the documenta foundation's catalogue especially. The actions organized by himself and other artists, such as Jörg Immendorf, KP Brehmer and Chris Reinecke, to denounce

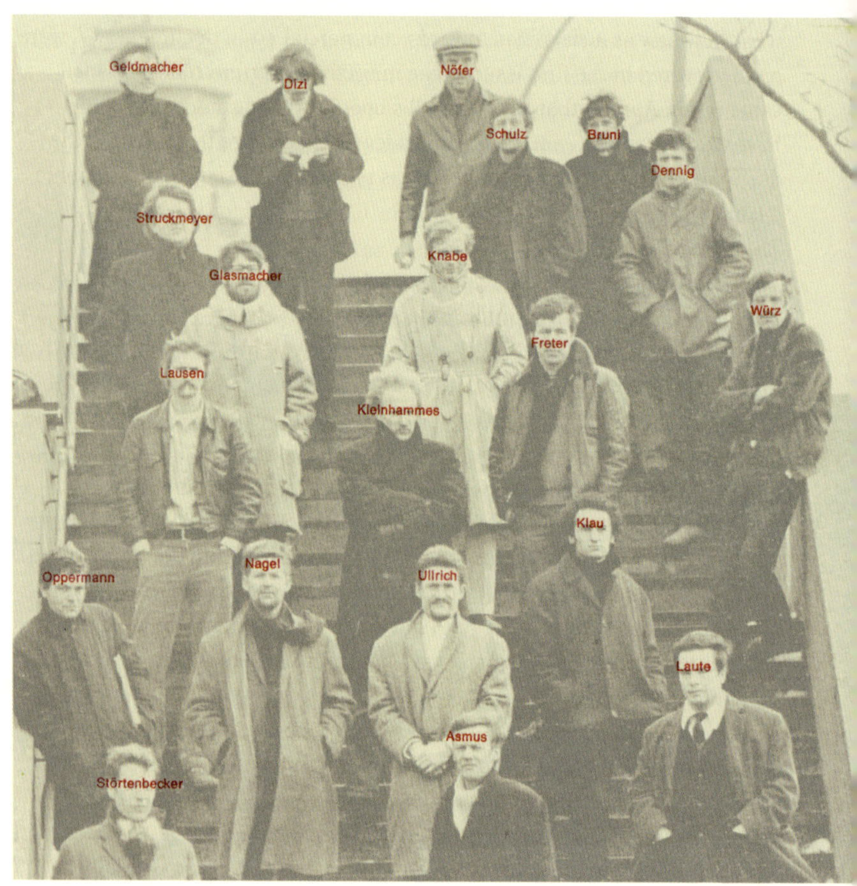

Some of the members of the Co-Op collective, an artists'
cooperative for the publication of multiples and graphic works.
Source: *Aktuelle Kunst in Hamburg*, Kunsthaus Hamburg, 1968.

[7] *Interfunktionen*, 1968-1975 (12 issues,
published annually or biannually).
Edited first by Friedrich W. Heubach
and then by Benjamin Buchloh.

[8] Georg Jappe, op. cit. While the cancellation of
Multimedia was attributed to a disagreement
with the sponsor – the WDR television
station – Jappe wondered in his article if
Vostell's criticism of Stünke had not played
a part in the decision to drop the event.

[9] George Brecht, 'Artists and Dealers'. In
Open, no. 2, Nice, May 1967, n.p.

[10] Ibid.

[11] Tomislav Laux, Bruno Bruni, Wolfgang
Oppermann, Hans-Jürgen Kleinhammes,
Konrad Schulz, Ernst Mitzka and Werner Nöfer.

[12] Upton Sinclair, *Co-Op. A Novel of Living
Together*. New York: Farrar and Rinehart, 1936.

what they saw as a clear bias towards commercial art in documenta IV, were amply covered in the first issue of the magazine *Interfunktionen*,[7] which came out in April of that year. Vostell's openly critical stance may well have worked against him when, only a few weeks before the opening, the documenta Board abruptly cancelled his proposed *Multimedia* programme, a happening and performance festival he had planned for the Municipal Theatre in Kassel.[8]

Similarly, George Brecht, another artist connected to Fluxus, had also recently criticised Stünke, in this case not for his cartelising influence but for the scant attention he gave to artists. In an article published in his short-lived magazine *Open*,[9] he and several other artists complained about the lack of communication (and payment) that characterised Galerie Der Spiegel. Brecht lamented that his dispatch of material, as requested by Stünke for the MAT Edition, had never been acknowledged: 'It was never communicated and nor were the letters sent to Mr. Stünke over the course of a year (in English, German and French) asking for information about it ever answered.' Wolf Vostell, he went on to say, had written to him saying, 'I told him again weeks ago that you want your books, but I have no influence over him. I did my first book with him in 1960... Same story! That fellow Stünke [...] he's not a bad chap, but he's from another generation, he has a different way of thinking.' Daniel Spoerri had told Brecht that he was experiencing a similar absence of communication and that 'little by little, I'm beginning to think that artists are the most trustworthy people on the planet, even if their reputation is the opposite'. 'Let's say it out loud,' Spoerri wrote in another letter Brecht reproduced in *Open:* 'Let's admit it: we are just producers of materials that a few blackmailers speculate with, but it is what it is...'[10]

The feeling of asphyxia that galleries' growing influence was beginning to provoke led others, meanwhile, to take the reins of distribution and advertise their own work independently of the art system. In the same year that documenta IV was held, a group of artists[11] – almost all of them students at the Hamburg School of Fine Arts – set up a cooperative they called 'Co-Op', taking inspiration from the title of a novel published in 1936 by the American author Upton Sinclair.[12] Sinclair's novel describes a social utopia in which workers take control of the production and distribution of goods and of the resulting capital gains. In a similar vein, Co-Op aspired to eschew the increasingly powerful and exclusionary networks and distribution circuits of the art market by bringing artistic production directly to interested parties and collectors. Said production included paintings but, above all, portfolios of graphic art. The profits from the first sales were used to publicise the initiative in the press and publish new portfolios of prints,

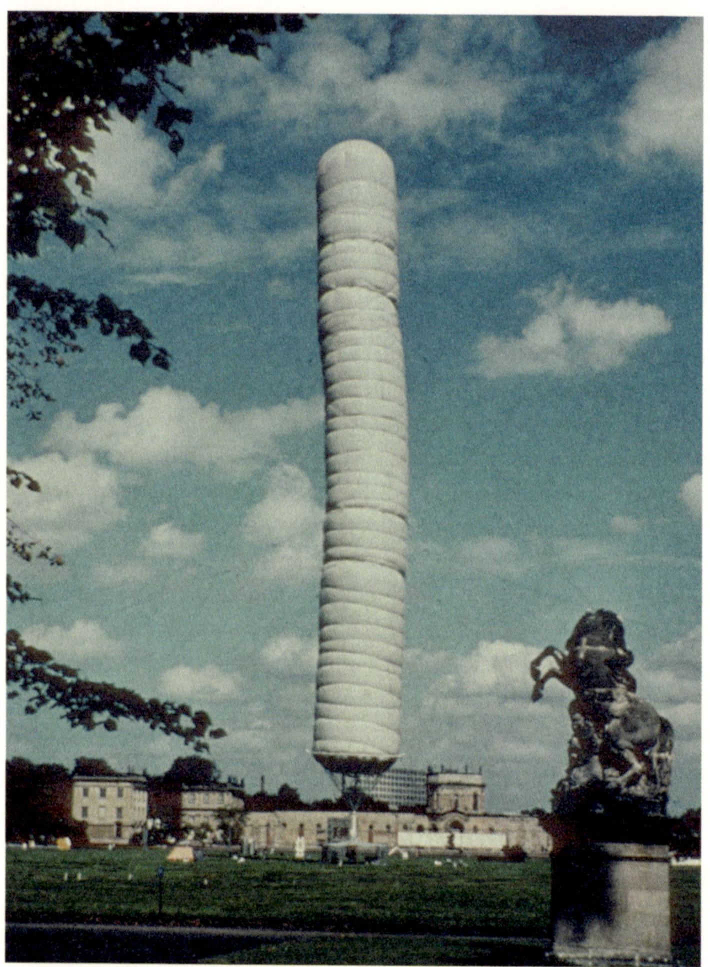

Christo and Jean-Claude, *5600 Cubic Meter Package*, 1968. The piece was part of the *Ambiente* section of documenta IV. Photo: documenta archiv.

13 *An alle* ['To all'], typed leaflet dated June 25, 1968, signed by students and teachers at the Hochschule für bildende Kunst in Hamburg. documenta archiv, AA, d4, 20, fol. 3.

14 The manifold protests and organisational chaos caused by Bode's peculiar working style were compounded by the departure of Werner Haftmann, due to a lack of understanding with the other members of the Board. He left documenta to become the first director of the Neue Nationalgalerie in Berlin.

created not only by members of the collective but also by other artists, including Anna Oppermann, Klaus Geldmacher, Sigmar Polke and Jan Voss. The cooperative did not last long, but long enough to stage a protest action on the opening day of the fourth documenta, in which they distributed leaflets to the public with a text that, once again, took aim at Hein Stünke: 'The entire American contribution (the importance of which is not in doubt) is selected by a Cologne-based gallery owner who, as a member of the documenta Board, finds himself in the unique position of being able to invite artists to participate and to acquire artwork for his gallery. This man is also responsible for organising Cologne's Art Fair, the association of so-called Progressives, and exhibitions like *ars multiplicata* (featuring items from his gallery whenever possible). Likewise, he also puts on exhibitions of German works by young artists for investment purposes, some of whom can expect to be 'adopted' by Stünke under socially repressive and exclusive contracts (those who have signed their first contracts with the gallery this year are lucky: Stünke has been able to include them all in documenta, or at least in the foundation's editions)...'[13]

If the spring of 1968 had been tricky at documenta IV,[14] by the end of the summer things were becoming distinctly thornier. The serious organisational problems experienced during the installation of the exhibition escalated during deinstallation, which, coupled with the criticism levelled at Arnold Bode ever since the first editions for his lack of budgetary acumen, would bring about his departure as artistic director. Feeling quite wretched, no doubt, Bode agreed to step aside, and soon after proposed as director of the next documenta the young Swiss curator Harald Szeemann, who had just resigned as head of the Kunsthalle in Bern because of the controversy ignited by his exhibition *When Attitudes Become Form* (1969).

***

From this point on, the evolution of documenta is, as they say, history, and widely known at that. documenta's organisational framework, artistic perspectives and working methods were entirely transformed by the change in artistic management, and nothing would ever be the same again. Indeed, not only did documenta's impact and public success weather the change; with this timely and much-needed overhaul, documenta consolidated its reputation which, as we know, has made it to the present day without buckling too much under the controversy – of all sorts, but mainly funding- and deficit-related – that has dogged each subsequent edition.

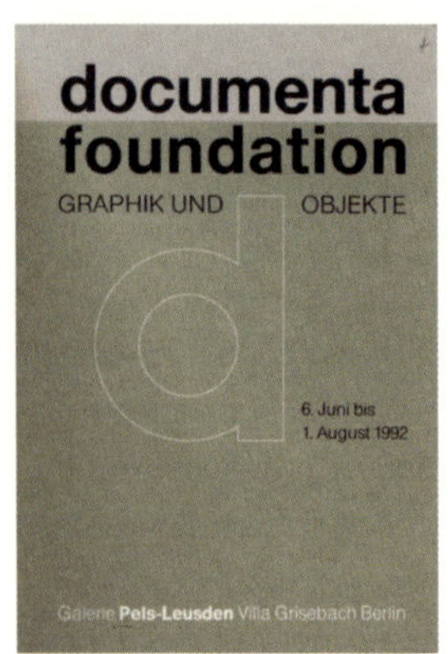

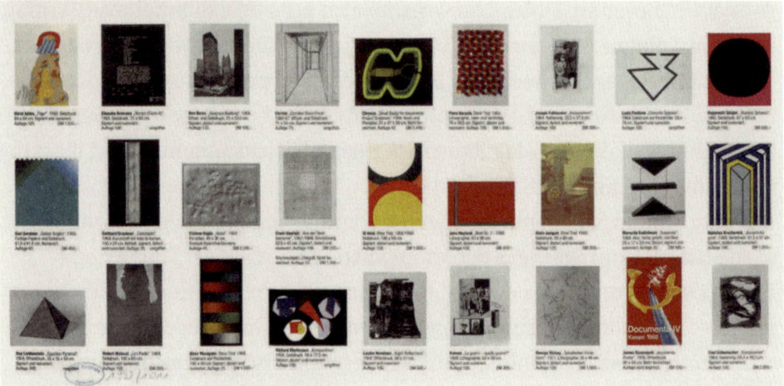

documenta foundation – Grafik und Objekte
[brochure], Galerie Peis-Leusden, Berlin, 1992.

---

[15] Minutes of the general meeting of the documenta foundation e.V., January 31, 1969. Zentralarchiv für Deutsche und Internationale Kunstmarktforschung - ZADIK, A1, IV, 004.

[16] Rolf-Gunter Dienst, op. cit., p. 10.

Nothing would ever be the same again for the documenta foundation either, although at the time it was hard to see the hurdles that lay ahead. After documenta IV, the trustees continued to work at their usual pace, which tended to slacken in the intervening years and intensify in the months leading up to each new exhibition. In 1969, after closing the accounts relative to its contributions to documenta IV (the funding of the impressive *Ambiente* section) and to the sales of its editions, which, once again had been very lucrative, the foundation convened to discuss the modification of certain practical aspects that would have only a modest strategic impact. Sales of the editions had been so successful that a 20% retail price hike was proposed, which would be applied only after galleries had had the chance to purchase copies, in a friendly gesture intended to ease tensions. A warehouse was hired in Cologne (with the firm Hasenkamp) to hold the stock which until then had been sitting at Galerie Der Spiegel. And lastly, ideas were discussed about possible forms of collaboration with the still far-off documenta 5.[15] As the minutes of the Board of Trustees' meetings show, any such collaboration would be contingent on the artistic direction of documenta's new chief curator, Harald Szeemann, so that for the time being, little more could be done than to wait for the programme to be defined.

However, things began to take a turn for the worse in 1970, when sales of the foundation's editions began to fall dramatically. The end of the 1960s was a turning point when art, like society, underwent a profound transformation. On the one hand, the radical conceptual and formal renovation of the art scene since the start of the decade was so far-reaching that its effects are still felt to this day. On the other, the galleries that had opened at the end of the 1950s had reached cruising speed by the middle of the decade, which meant that not only were there more galleries, but their share of power had multiplied exponentially. While collecting was clearly gaining ground, galleries were progressing in leaps and bounds and consequently the documenta foundation now had a great deal more competition.

Hein Stünke was quick to spot some of these changes, which he outlined in 1972: 'The growth of the art prints market in Germany is [also] interesting in this context. Years ago, especially at the first, second and third [Cologne] fairs, it was burgeoning. Although it is still a crucial part of any gallery, it has now declined. Of course, the reason for this cannot be that demand is now covered; there are many things at play. The volume of production is higher but not better, and customers have noticed this. Moreover, the circle of buyers cannot expand continuously. Opening up new circles of interest requires many years' work...'[16]

Clearly, the question of quality Stünke alludes to depends greatly on subjective appreciation. But, interestingly, neither he nor his fellow trustees seem to have considered an aspect which, today, cannot fail to catch our attention: throughout its trajectory, the documenta foundation worked with artists who, save the odd exception, remained within the canons of classical genres (painting, sculpture, drawing), while all around other artists were seeking to break out of these moulds and approach 'serial' or 'published' artwork from new angles, often with the desire to short-circuit the power of absorption the art market was increasingly displaying. The genealogy of the more experimental artists' publications, as we know them today, goes back precisely to the early 1960s, and although many of the genre's early pioneers (Daniel Spoerri, Dieter Roth and Wolf Vostell, to name only the most prominent) orbited in the same circles and would no doubt have been easily approachable, their practice must have fallen outside the foundation's interests as they were never invited to participate in the project.

The new artistic leadership of documenta might have brought a breath of fresh air to the conservative selection criteria of the documenta foundation. In May 1971, Harald Szeemann and Jean Christophe Amman attended a meeting of the documenta foundation's Board of Trustees, which took place, as was often the case, in the main office of Galerie Der Spiegel in Richartzstrasse in Cologne. Szeemann and Amman presented a list of fifty artists as candidates for a possible 'Edition 72' of the documenta foundation and suggested that the latter should also offer artists' books and records at the exhibition, besides editions and prints.[17] Neither proposal came to fruition. The increasing lack of understanding between the trustees and Szeemann and his team, coupled with Arnold Bode's meddling (keen as he was to rekindle his influence within documenta and keep his ties with board members), and the foundation's own growing desire to play a role in the

[17] Minutes of the general meeting of the documenta foundation e.V., May 7, 1971. documenta archive, AA, d5, 117a, fol. 76-83.

[18] Minutes of the general meeting of the documenta foundation e.V., September 16, 1977. Zentralarchiv für Deutsche und Internationale Kunstmarktforschung - ZADIK, A1, IV, 005.

[19] Minutes of the meeting of the members of the documenta foundation, September 16, 1977, p. 8. Zentralarchiv des deutschen und internationalen Kunstforschung - ZADIK, A1, IV, 005.

[20] 'Pop / minimalism / Color Field / sculpture / Artists & Photographs / Art & Language / idea, process, concept / independent categories / video, film, photography / music.'

definition of the documenta programme, made for constant disagreements. The foundation never succeeded in executing any new editions for documenta 5. Its main contribution to the 1972 exhibition, by no means negligible, was the financing of Ed Kienholz's breathtaking installation *Five Car Stud*, which had to be shipped from America, costing considerably more than Szeemann's budget could have afforded.

From 1972, the tensions between documenta's trustees and its artistic team were endless, and the foundation started to step back, never to return. There was no understanding with Karl Ruhrberg and Wieland Schmied, who had been appointed to conceive the documenta 6 programme but ended up quitting and being replaced by Manfred Schneckenburger. With Schneckenburger, and especially with Rudolf Lukas, documenta's new financial manager – the first to do the job full-time – tensions remained high. What did decrease, and irrevocably, was the foundation's income from the sale of editions. From 1972, sales were outsourced, first to Galerie Wilbrand in Bonn and then to Galerie Peis-Leusden in Berlin, in the hope that professional dedication would stimulate revenue, but the attempt was futile. In the mid-1970s the foundation was presented with the chance to cultivate contacts with other galleries with a view to possible collaborations, in particular with Multiples, Inc. which Marian Goodman had founded in New York in 1965, but the Board of Trustees declined, considering Goodman's demanding conditions to be unprofitable and therefore unacceptable.

In June 1976, Herbert von Buttlar, president of the foundation since its creation and member of the documenta team, died unexpectedly.[18] In the spring of 1977, Arnold Bode informed the foundation that Philip Rosenthal had expressed a desire to revive collaboration, but the opportunity was truncated by Bode's death in October 1977, just after the close of documenta 6. Gradually, the individuals who had been instrumental in articulating the relationship between the foundation and documenta began to disappear, which only debilitated ties further.

The minutes of the meeting of the Board of Trustees held in September 1977 include an interesting proposal which, had it been carried out, would have radically shaken up the foundation's editorial approach.[19] The artists that were put forward for consideration in anticipation of the next edition had been grouped under ten thematic headings, and many of them shared a new way of conceiving publications that veered away from the traditions of painting and printmaking and embraced more contemporary postulates:[20] Ed Ruscha, Dieter Roth, John Baldessari, Richard Long, Hanna Darvoben and Michael Snow, among many others. The desire for renewal,

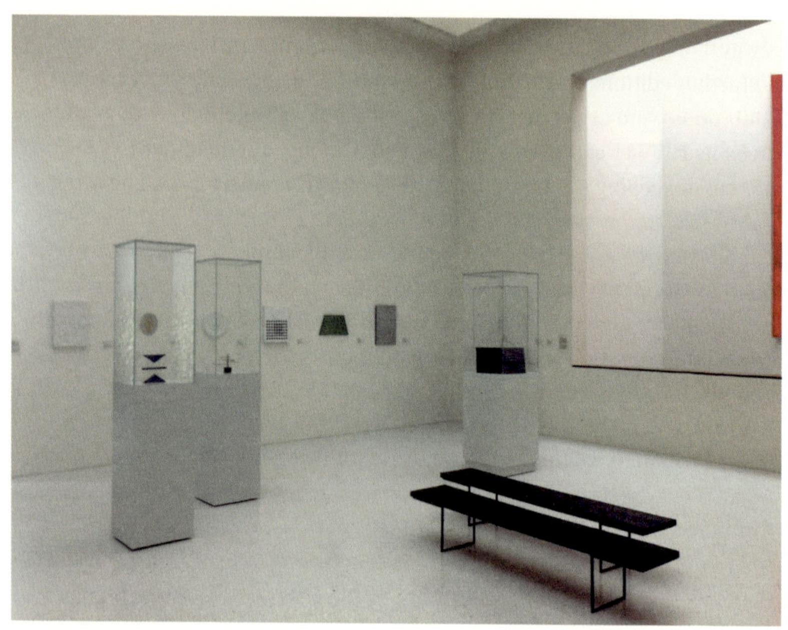

Editions of the documenta foundation on view in the
exhibition *about: documenta*, Neue Galerie, Kassel, 2020.
Photo: Mela Dávila Freire.

21 *documenta foundation,* Sparkasse Kassel
exhibition hall, June–September 1977; and
documenta foundation: Grafik und Objekte,
Galerie Peis-Leusden, Berlin, June–August 1992.

however, came too late. Gradually, the foundation's activity waned.
No further editions were brought out after 1968, and only a few more
exhibitions were organised.[21] Even so, some talks were held with Rudi
Fuchs in 1979 to explore possible collaborations, but documenta's
interest in keeping the relationship alive had completely died. The strain
of the disharmony between the new documenta organisers and the 'old
school' trustees was too entrenched, as was the dubious reputation of
the foundation, plagued as it was by conflicts of interest, and by the
suspicion – to an extent, founded – that they offered financial sponsorship
only on the condition that they retained their capacity to influence the
programming of content.

Epilogue: the end and a new beginning?

The boundary between institutional art exhibition and art market, as we perceive it today, began to crystallise around 1968 in documenta and in the West generally. It is no coincidence that this was the year that the Venice Biennale definitively closed its sales office, as already mentioned. Although there would be no going back from this development, there remained certain pockets of resistance inside documenta. On the one hand, the documenta foundation was not to be moved from its conviction that as a generator of revenue, it was entitled to hold sway over matters of content – a conviction that would only hasten the estrangement between the foundation and documenta's curatorial team as preparations got underway for documenta 5. On the other, art dealers would continue to engage in sporadic attempts to derive commercial gain from the Kassel exhibition. The most significant of these attempts took place in the summer of 1972 when a group of Cologne galleries rented a building in the city to exhibit and sell artwork to coincide with documenta 5. However, the initiative failed to produce the desired results and was never repeated.

The final breakdown of the close collaboration between documenta and the art trade – hitherto represented in Kassel by the documenta foundation and in particular by Hein Stünke – was one of several major changes that affected the 1972 exhibition in the matter of funding. When the exhibition closed, the inflated deficit prompted documenta GmbH to point the finger directly at Szeemann in an attempt to hold him responsible for the poor financial results. While the ensuing judicial resolution of the conflict exonerated the artistic director from personal liability, the incident served to bring about further, wider-reaching consequences: state funding was secured for future documenta exhibitions, a stable full-time professional team was put in charge of the financial management of the project, and, above all, *die Freiheit des Ausstellungsmachers* – that is, the artistic freedom of the curatorial team – was safeguarded.

Ever since, artistic freedom, not only for artists but also for curators, has been upheld as one of the distinguishing pillars of the documenta project. But what does artistic freedom really mean and what are its limits? The definition, while neither univocal nor fixed, has given rise to many different interpretations, as evinced by the various forms that the tension between artistic creation and market pressure have taken over the years. The conflicts of interest at the heart of documenta which this book addresses illustrate this tension. One must remember that these conflicts were playing out against the backdrop of the Cold War, that is, amid the power struggle between two opposing models of political and economic organisation. Boris Groys claims that a work of art is presented to the public in one of two ways: either as merchandise or as propaganda, and that during the period following World War II the first of these two options gained the upper hand: 'After the end of World War II and especially after the change of regime in the former socialist Eastern European countries, the commercial system of art production and distribution dominated the political system. The notion of art became almost synonymous with the notion of the art market, so that the art produced under non-market conditions was de facto excluded from the field of institutionally recognised art.'[1] On the other side of the Wall, meanwhile, the 'free market' championed by Western Europe was seen as an illusion, a complot by which a privileged few could retain almost monopoly control of the art trade.[2] Back in documenta, Hein Stünke was analysing the matter with his usual pragmatism and concluding that the positions on either side of the Wall were in fact not so distant: 'The work of art as a commodity exists with socialists and with capitalists: both sell art, only the forms of distribution are different. The commercial aspect of art is the same. Both demand money and charge for distribution. Commodities can be herrings as well as works of art.'[3]

In view of the tension between artistic creation and commercial pressure, it is possible to apprehend each documenta exhibition as a renewed endeavour to open up a space of freedom in which art that is not institutionally recognised, and therefore not yet absorbed by the market, can find a place. Yet paradoxically, the closer documenta gets to achieving this goal, the more it reinforces its institutional character and so the more elusive it becomes. Can this vicious circle be broken? Perhaps, but it is certainly not easy. Each new edition of documenta, almost without exception, has strived to reinvent itself in its determination to overcome this contradiction, which has involved fending off the various attacks the project regularly comes in for, which most of the time boil down to one thing: a criticism of the principle of artistic freedom.

Mission and Commission is being released at precisely the moment that documenta is about to open its fifteenth edition, which promises to be the most successful in terms of its evasion of market pressure, thanks

---

[1] Boris Groys, *Art Power*. Massachussets: MIT Press, 2008, p. 5.

[2] See Walter Hänel, *Maler, Mäzene, Monopole. Zur Kunstpolitik in Westdeutschland*. East Berlin: Dietzt Verlag, 1967. Alexia Pooth is currently preparing *Exhibiton Politics. Die documenta und die DDR* for publication, a study on how documenta was viewed from East Germany, which will undoubtedly prove illuminating in this respect.

[3] Rolf-Gunter Dienst, interview with Hein Stünke, op. cit., p. 8.

to a radical choice of agents and practices. Almost without exception, the selected proposals are redefining what it means to 'be an artist' and 'make art' through a combination of aesthetic output and social and political activism and avoiding being absorbed by the art market and galleries. The vicious attacks, however, have already begun. While the pretexts of these attacks may seem new or original, once again, it is artistic freedom that underlies the debate. This debate would undoubtedly be enriched by a better and deeper understanding of the history and evolution of the concept of artistic freedom that inspires documenta; but for now, *Mission and Commission* aspires to advance the process of historical revision that will hopefully find continuity in many other future works of research.

Bibliography

'Documenta: Kunst zu billigen Preisen'. In *Hessische Allgemeine*, 118, 1964, documenta archiv, AA, d03, 5.

'Spenden', undated list [1955], documenta archiv, AA, d01, 16, fol. 141.

Aktuelle Kunst in Hamburg. Hamburg: Kunsthaus Hamburg, 1968.

An alle, typed leaflet dated June 25, 1968, signed by students and teachers at the Hochschule für bildende Kunst in Hamburg, documenta archiv, AA, d4, 20, fol. 3.

Annual accounts documenta & Fridericianum 1968-1997, documenta archiv, AA.

ars multiplicata: Vervielfältigte Kunst seit 1945, press release, Historisches Archiv der Stadt Köln – HASTK, inventory no. 1968 [Kölnischer Kunstverein], ACC500-A12.

ars multiplicata: Vervielfältigte Kunst seit 1945. Cologne: Kölnischer Kunstverein, 1968.

ars porcellana, Historisches Archiv der Stadt Köln – HASTK, inventory no. 1386 [Kölnischer Kunstverein], ACC500-A12.

Barr, Alfred H., Jr., 'Is Modern Art Communistic? On the contrary, says an expert, it is damned in Soviet Russia as it was in Nazi Germany'. In *The New York Times Magazine*, December 14, 1952, p. 22.

Barreiro López, Paula [ed.], *Atlántico Frío. Historias transnacionales del arte y la política en los tiempos del telón de acero.* Madrid: Brumaria, 2019.

Behnke, Edith and Josephine Gabler [eds.], *ars porcellana - Die Rosenthal Relief Reihe*. Wörlen: Museum Moderner Kunst, 2009.

Benkhe, Edith, *Limitierte Kunstobjekte in Porzellan, 1968-2003*, doctoral dissertation, Faculty of Philosophy of the Rheinische Friedrich-Wilhelms Universität, Bonn, 2011.

Beuckers, Klaus Gereon, Hans-Edwin Friedich and Sven Hanuschek [eds.], *Wolf Vostell: Dé-coll/age als Manifest, Manifest als Dé-coll/age. Manifeste, Aktionsvorträge, Essays*. Munich: edition text + kritik - Richard Boorberg Verlag, 2014.

Blase, Karl Oskar, introduction to a video interview with Willi Bongard in the context of documenta 5, Kassel, 1972. ZKM - Center for Art and Media Karlsruhe, Archive Audiovisual documentation of documenta 5.

Bode, Arnold, 'Bode-Plan', cover letter with exposé to the Mayor of Kassel, January 19, 1954, documenta archiv, AA, d01, 20, fol. 8-12.

Bode, Arnold in an anonymous interview, sound recording, c. 1964, documenta archiv [3002490_DIGdA_2_09].

Bode, Arnold, letter to Toni Feldenkirchen, December 16, 1967, Historisches Archiv der Stadt Köln – HASTK, inventory no. 1968 [Kölnischer Kunstverein], ACC500-A12.

Bode, Arnold [ed.], *ars porcellana*. Cologne: Kölnischer Kunstverein, 1968.

Bode, Peter M., 'Das Kunstwerk im Zeitalter seiner technischen Multiplizierbarkeit. Zur Ausstellung *ars multiplicata* in der Kunsthalle Köln'. In *Kölner Stadt-Anzeiger*, January 25, 1968.

Bongard, Willi, *Kunst und Kommerz: zwischen Passion und Spekulation*. Oldenburg: Stalling Verlag, 1967.

Bongard, Willi, 'Was kostet die Documenta? Eine Selbsthilfereaktion stösst auf Kritik'. In *Die Zeit*, no. 20, April 17, 1968.

Bongard, Willi, 'Markt für 100 Tage'. In *Die Zeit*, no. 29, July 19, 1968, p. 27.

Bongard, Willi, 'Gute Geschäfte mit Grafik'. In *Die Zeit*, no. 33, August 16, 1968, p. 28, documenta archiv, AA, d04, 12.

Bongard, Willi, *Kunstkompass*, 1970.

Brecht, George, 'Artists and Dealers'. In *Open*, no. 2, Nice, May 1967.

Buckermann, Paul, *Die Vermessung der Kunstwelt. Quantifizierende Beobachtungen und plurale Ordnungen der Kunst*. Weilerswist: Velbrück Wissenschaft, 2020.

Buttlar, Herbert von, untitled text, undated [1968]. Zentralarchiv für Deutsche und internationale Kunstmarktforschung - ZADIK, A1, IV, 004.

Cabañas Bravo, Miguel, *La Primera Bienal Hispanoamericana de Arte: Arte, política y polémica en un certamen internacional de los años cincuenta*. Doctoral dissertation, Universidad Complutense de Madrid, 1991. [http://hdl.handle.net/10261/11455, retrieved in January 2022]

Corlett, Mary Lee (ed.), *The Prints of Roy Lichtenstein: A Catalogue Raisonné 1948-1993*. New York: National Gallery of Art / Hudson Hills, 1994.

Court of Audit of the State of Hessen. Audit of the use of federal and state subsidies granted for the realisation of the documenta II art exhibition. Darmstadt, 'Conclusion and execution of contracts' [item 6c], September 4, 1961, p. 10, documenta archiv, AA, d02, 51.

Dienst, Rolf-Gunter, 'Interview mit Hein Stünke'. In *Das Kunstwerk. Zeitschrift für bildende Kunst*, no. 6, November 1972, pp. 8-10.

documenta foundation – Edition 64 [brochure]. Kassel: documenta foundation, 1964.

documenta foundation [exhibition brochure, Sparkasse Kassel]. Kassel: documenta foundation, 1977.

documenta foundation, e. V. [brochure]. Kassel: documenta foundation, 1977.

documenta foundation: Grafik und Objekte [exhibition brochure]. Berlin: Galerie Peis-Leusden, 1992.

Eckstein, Hans, 'Unsere Gegenstände - Zur Eröffnung der Design-Documenta'. In *form*, no. 27, 1964.

Fehrlin, Gisela, 'Kasseler Kunst-Messe, 1959'. In *Deutsche Rundschau*, Baden-Baden, December 1959.

Fleckner, Uwe (ed.), *Angriff auf die Avantgarde. Kunst und Kunstpolitik im Nationalsozialismus*. Munich: De Gruyter Akademie Forschung, 2007.

Fleckner, Uwe and Uwe M. Schneede (eds.), *Bürgerliche Avantgarde. 200 Jahre Kunstverein Hamburg*. Berlin: Hatje Cantz, 2017.

Fourest, Henry-Pierre, *Die europäische Keramik. Porzellan - Steingut - Fayence*. Freiburg: Herder, 1983.

Franke, Anselm, Nida Ghouse, Paz Guevara, and Antonia Majaca (eds.), *Parapolitics: Cultural Freedom and the Cold War*. Berlin: Haus der Kulturen der Welt and Sternberg Press, 2021.

Garnatz, Eberhard, interview with Hein Stünke [unpublished], September 15, 1970, Zentralarchiv für Deutsche und Internationale Kunstmarktforschung – ZADIK, A1, IV, 002.

Geldmacher, Klaus and Francesco Mariotti, *Projekt Geldmacher Mariotti – 4. Documenta* [brochure]. Kassel: self-published, 1968.

Gentile, Carlo, 'Der Krieg des Dr. Haftmann'. In *Süddeutsche Zeitung*, June 6, 2021.

Georgsdorf, Heiner (ed.), *Arnold Bode, Schriften und Gespräche*. Kassel and Frankfurt: documenta archiv and Siebenhaar Verlag 2007.

Gerstner, Karl and Henri Stierlin (ed.), *Der Geist der Farbe. Karl Gerstner und seine Kunst*. Stuttgart: Deutsche Verlags-Anstalt (DVA), 1981.

Gerstner, Karl and Daniel Spoerri (eds.), *Kunstwerke, die bewegen, die sich bewegen oder bewegen lassen. Multiplizierte demokratische Kunst und Originale in Serien aus den 60n Jahren*. Cologne: Galerie Der Spiegel, 1993.

Gross, Raphael, Lars Bang Larsen, Dorlis Blume, Alexia Pooth, Julia Voss and Dorothee Wierling (eds.), *documenta: Politics and Art*. Berlin: Deutsches Historisches Museum and Prestel Verlag, 2021.

Groys, Borys, 'The Cold War between the Medium and the Message: Western Modernism vs Socialist Realism'. In *e-flux Journal*, no. 104, November 2019.

Haftmann, Werner, *Malerei im zwanzigsten Jahrhundert*. Munich: Prestel Verlag, 1954.

Handberg, Kristian, 'The Shock of the Contemporary: documenta II and the Louisiana Museum'. In *On Curating*, no. 33. [https://www.on-curating.org/issue-33-reader/the-shock-of-the-contemporary-documenta-ii-and-the-louisiana-museum.html#_edn9, retrieved in January 2022]

Hänel, Walter, *Maler, Mäzene, Monopole. Zur Kunstpolitik in Westdeutschland*. East Berlin: Dietzt Verlag, 1967.

Hennig, Arno, letter to the Society for Western Art of the Twentieth Century, December 24, 1954, documenta archiv, AA, d01, 20, fol. 102.

Heubach, Friedrich W. [first period] and Buchloh, Benjamin [second period] [eds.], *Interfunktionen*, 1968-1975.

Holzträger, Hans, *Kampfeinsatz der Hitler Jugend im Chaos der letzten Kriegsmonate*. Dinklage: AGK Verlag, 1995.

Honisch, Dieter et al. (eds.), *Die Rosenthal Story*. Düsseldorf: Econ Verlag, 1980.

Honnef, Klaus, 'Kunsthistorische Missverständnisse. Kölner Ausstellung *ars multiplicata* viel unzulänglich aus'. In *Aachenen Nachrichten - 'Das Feuilleton'*, January 27, 1968.

Honnef, Klaus and Hans M. Schmidt (eds.), *Aus den Trummern. Kunst und Kultur im Rheinland und Westfalen 1945 – 1952*. Cologne: Rheinland-Verlag, 1985.

Jappe, Georg, 'Im Hintergrund der Documenta. Gericht der Künstler und Boykott der Kunsthändler'. In *Frankfurter Allgemeine Zeitung*, May 13, 1968, documenta archiv, AA, d04, 3.

Jensen, Knud W., *Mein Louisiana Leben. Werdegang eines Museums*. Klagenfurt: Ritter Verlag, 1991.

Joos, Birgit, Philipp Oswalt and Daniel Tyradellis (eds.), *Bauhaus Documenta. Vision und Marke*. Leipzig: Spector Books, 2019.

Kahl, Eva, *Dürer-Nachfolge in der Reliefplastik unter besonderer Berücksichtigung des Eichstätter Meisters Loy Hering*. Doctoral dissertation, Universität Erlangen, 1940.

Kårstner, Erhart, *Maler machen Bücher*. Kassel: Kunstverein, 1968.

Keller, Sven, *Volksgemeinschaft am Ende: Gesellschaft und Gewalt 1944-1945*. Quellen und Darstellungen zur Zeitgeschichte, vol. 97. Munich: De Gruyter, 2013.

Kimpel, Harald, *documenta: Mythos und Wirklichkeit*. Cologne: Dumont Buchverlag, 1997.

Leering, Jean, internal report [1968]. Zentralarchiv für Deutsche und Internationale Kunstmarktforschung - ZADIK, A1, IV, 004.

Lemke, Heinz, letter to Ludwig Preller, April 7, 1954, documenta archiv, AA, d01, 20, fol. 33/34.

Lemke, Heinz, letter to the Magistrate of the City of Kassel, July 23, 1954, documenta archiv, AA, d01, 20, fol. 65-68.

Lemke, Heinz, letter to Theodor Heuss, August 16, 1954, documenta archiv, AA, Kassel, d01, 20, fol. 75.

Lemke, Heinz, letter to Ludwig Preller, December 11, 1954, documenta archiv, AA, d01, 20, fol. 99.

Mavignier, Almir, letter to Arnold Bode, June 13, 1966, Arnold Bode documenta archiv estate, 126, fol. 65.

Mies van der Rohe, Ludwig, 'Museum for a Small City'. In *Architectural Forum* no. 78, 1943.

Minutes of the meeting of the documenta GmbH, January 17, 1961, documenta archiv, AA, d03, 72, fol. 4-15.

Minutes of the meeting of the documenta Supervisory Board, January 23, 1962, documenta archiv, AA, d03, 70, fol. 165-169.

Minutes of the general meeting of the documenta foundation e.V., July 24, 1964, Zentralarchiv für Deutsche und Internationale Kunstmarktforschung - ZADIK, Al, IV, 004.

Minutes of the general meeting of the documenta foundation, October 27, 1964, Zentralarchiv für Deutsche und Internationale Kunstmarktforschung - ZADIK, A1, IV, 004.

Minutes of the general meeting of the documenta foundation e.V., July 21, 1967, Zentralarchiv für Deutsche und Internationale Kunstmarktforschung - ZADIK, A1, IV, 004.

Minutes of the general meeting of the documenta foundation e.V., January 31, 1969. Zentralarchiv für Deutsche und Internationale Kunstmarktforschung - ZADIK, A1, IV, 004.

Minutes of the general meeting of the documenta foundation e.V., May 7, 1971. documenta archive, AA, d5, 117a, fol. 76-83.

Minutes of the general meeting of the documenta foundation e.V., September 16, 1977. Zentralarchiv für Deutsche und Internationale Kunstmarktforschung - ZADIK, A1, IV, 005.

Mit Kunst Leben. Hommage Philip Rosenthal. Selb: Rosenthal AG, 2003.

Øberg-Pedersen, F. W., letter to Knud Jensen, May 29, 1969, Archive of the Louisiana Museum of Modern Art, Humblebæck.

Peters, Olaf (ed.), *Degenerate Art. The Attack on Modern Art in Nazi Germany, 1937*. New York: Prestel and Neue Galerie - Museum for German and Austrian Art, 2014.

Pfeiffer-Belli, Erich, ,Industrieform und Plakat. Eine Ausstellung anlässlich der Kasseler documenta III'. In *Süddeutsche Zeitung*, August 28, 1964, documenta archiv, AA, d03, 10.

Rathke, Edward, 'Ring frei in Kassel'. In *Artis*, no. 2, February 1968, pp. 10-13.

Reppin, Ursula, video interview, *Audioarchivkunst*. [http://audioarchivkunst.de/zeitzeugen/ursula-reppin/, retrieved in September 2021]

Resolution addressed to the Reich Treasurer of the Hitler Jugend, relative to the request for funds by way of compensation for services rendered by Hein Stünke in the Hitler Jugend, 22 September 1942, Federal Archives of Germany, Koblenz (BArch R 9361-II/ 998878].

Reyburn, Scott, 'At Venice Biennale, the Art's for Sale, if You Know the Right People'. In *The New York Times*, May 14, 2019.

Riedmann, Mirl, 'Das Flüstern der Fussnoten'. In *documenta Studies*, no. 09, June 2020. [https://documenta-studien.de/media/1/documenta_studien_9_Mirl_Redmann.pdf, retrieved in January 2022]

Rosenthal, Philip, letter to Almir Mavignier, July 28, 1966, Arnold Bode documenta archiv estate, 126, fol. 51.

Saunders, Frances Stonor, *Who Paid the Piper? The CIA and the Cultural Cold War*. London: Granta, 1999.

Schelsky, Helmut, *Die skeptische Generation. Eine Soziologie der deutschen Jugend*. Düsseldorf and Cologne: Eugen Diederichs Verlag, 1957.

Schieder, Martin, *Im Blick des anderen: Die deutsch-französischen Kunstbeziehungen 1945-1959*. Freiburg: De Gruyter, 2005.

Schmidt, Katharina, 'Geh durch den Spiegel. Laudatio anlässlich der Verleihung des Art Cologne-Preses 1991 an Hein Stünke'. In *Sediment*, no. 1. Bonn: Zentral Archiv für Deutsche und Internationale Kunstmarktforschung, 1994, pp. 15-20.

Schmidt, Regina, 'Die Galerie Der Spiegel und der Bundesdeutsche Markt'. In *Sediment*, no. 1. Bonn: Zentral Archiv für Deutsche und Internationale Kunstmarktforschung, 1994, pp. 21-24.

Schmied, Wieland, 'Kunst & Kommerz. Staunend auf dem Markt'. In *Der Spiegel*, March 17, 1968.

Schultz, Jürgen, *Die Akademie für Jugendführung der Hitlerjugend in Braunschweig*, Braunschweiger Werkstücke, Reihe A, vol. 15. Braunschweig: Stadtarchiv und Stadtbibliothek and Weisenhaus Buchdruckerei, 1978.

Siemen, Wilhelm [ed.], *Begegnungen - Zeitgenössische Porzellanplastik*. Hohemberger an der Eger: Deutsches Porzellan Museum, 1999.

Sinclair, Upton, *Co-Op. A Novel of Living Together*. New York: Farrar and Rinehart, 1936.

Spoerri, Daniel [ed.], *Material. Zeitschrift für konkrete Dichtung und bildende Kunst*, 1958 - 1960.

Stachelhaus, Heiner, 'Köln wird zum Kunsthandelszentrum'. In *Ruhr Nachrichten*, January 27, 1967.

Statutes of the association 'Circle of Friends of documenta', undated, documenta archiv, AA, d02, 38, fol. 17-23.

Statutes of the documenta forum, adopted and signed June 16, 1972, documenta archiv, AA, d05, 120.

Statutes of the documenta foundation e. V. [first version], October 27, 1964, documenta archiv, AA, d04, 31, fol. 46-50.

Statutes of the documenta foundation e. V. [second version], undated, Zentralarchiv für Deutsche und Internationale Kunstmarktforschung - ZADIK, A1, IV, 004.

Stoph, Willi, letter to the Mayor of the City of Kassel, January 10, 1955, documenta archiv, AA, d01, 20, fol. 103/104.

Stünke, Hein [ed.], *Kampf und Glaube: Gedichte österreichischer Dichter, 1933-1938*. Potsdam: Ludwig Voggenreiter Verlag, 1938.

Stünke, Hein, letter to Franz Tumler, July 20, 1940, Deutsches Literaturarchiv Marbach, A: Tumler, Franz D - 92.4.891.

Stünke, Hein, 'Die Akademie für Jugendführung'. In *Westermanns Monatshefte*, July 1944.

Stünke, Hein, letter to Franz Tumler, July 27, 1947, Deutsches Literaturarchiv Marbach, A: Tumler, Franz D - 92.4.891.

Stünke, Hein, 'Arnold Bode'. In *Jahresring 78-79. Literatur und Kunst der Gegenwart*. Stuttgart: Deutsche Verlags-Anstalt, 1978, p. 266-271.

Sturm, Birgit Maria, 'Diese diffizile Ware Kunst. Ein Interview mit dem Kölner Galeristen Hein Stünke über die Entstehungsgeschichte des Kölner Kunstmarktes'. In *Art Position*, year 5, no. 22, 1993, pp. 20-33.

Troeger, Heinrich, letter to the Society for Western Art of the Twentieth Century, January 25, 1955, documenta archiv, AA, d01, 20, fol. 107.

Vatsella, Katerina, *Edition MAT: Die Entstehung einer Kunstform*. Bremen: H. M. Hauschild, 1998.

Vowinckel, Andreas and Harald Kimpel, *Die documenta foundation. Ein Modell der Selbstfinanzierung*. Marburg: Jonas Verlag, 2002.

Vowinckel, Andreas, letter on behalf of the documenta foundation to André Emmerich, Cologne, March 6, 1968, Zentralarchiv für Deutsche und Internationale Kunstmarktforschung - ZADIK, A1, IV, 002.

Werner Schmalenbach. Cologne: Verlag der Buchhandlung Walther König, 2011, p. 45.

Z., G., 'ars porcellana?' In *Frankfurter Allgemeine Zeitung*, no. 213, September 13, 1968.

Zentralarchiv für Deutsche und Internationale Kunstmarktforschung - ZADIK [ed.], *Art Cologne: Die Erste aller Kunstmessen / The First Art Fair*. Cologne: ZADIK and Verlag der Buchhandlung Walther König, 2016, p. 41.

Zwirner, Rudolf, *Ich wollte immer Gegenwart. Autobiographie* [with Nicola Kuhn]. Cologne: Wienand Verlag, 2019.

Zwirner, Rudolf, letter on behalf of the Association of German Progressive Art Galleries to Hein Stünke, April 5, 1968, documenta archiv, AA, d04, 31, fol. 86.

About the author

Mela Dávila Freire's interest lies in publishing as an artistic genre, with a particular focus on the conceptual and physical intersection between contemporary art and archives. Her work encompasses researching, writing, curating and lecturing, in particular about artist's publications and experimental publishing. She also develops organizational models for the management of archival collections in museums and art archives, aiming to facilitate public access, increase visibility and establish a good connectivity with art collections.

Among others, she has collaborated with Museu d'Art Contemporani de Barcelona – MACBA, Museo Reina Sofía (Madrid), documenta archive (Kassel - Germany), Museum of German History (Berlin - Germany), Lafuente Archive (Santander - Spain), Universidad de las Artes (Guayaquil - Ecuador), Academy of Art and Design FHNW - Institute of Experimental Design / Critical Media Lab (Basel, Switzerland) and Cuenca Biennale (Cuenca, Ecuador).

Mela Dávila Freire holds a degree in English and German Literature and Language, and is currently a doctoral candidate at the Hamburg School of Fine Arts – HfbK. She was a resident of the Paul Klee Summer Academy at the Bern Academy of the Arts – HKB in Bern from 2022 to 2023.

Colophon

Mission and Commission: documenta and the Art Market 1955 - 1968
Mela Dávila Freire

Translation, Stéphanie Jennings
Design and layout, Cosmic, Barcelona. www.cosmic.es
Color separation, Maria Coll Sagué
Proofreading, Christopher Foster
Printing and binding, Gráficas Rodés

© of this edition, 2022 Polígrafa, Barcelona. www.poligrafa.com
© of the text and translation, the author and the translator
© of the photographs, documenta archiv, Kassel / Günther Becker, Wolfgang Haut, Werner
Kohn, Klaus Meiner-Ude; Stadtarchiv, Kassel / Friedrich Unkel; Bundesarchiv, Koblenz / Teubner;
Historiathek, Munich; Louisiana Museum of Modern Art Archive; Photostiftung Schweiz, Zurich
/ Rudolf Lichtsteiner; Galerie Der Spiegel / Dr. Salchow; Angelika Platen, Berlin; Archive of
Rosenthal AG, Selb; Photografische Galerie Hartzenbusch, Köln; Die Zeit Archive, Hamburg

First edition

ISBN: 9788434314818
Dep legal. B-26247 – 2022

Available in the USA and Canada through
D.A.P. / Distributed Art Publishers
75 Broad Street, Suite 630, New York, NY 10004.
Tel: (212) 627-1999 · Fax: (212) 627-9484

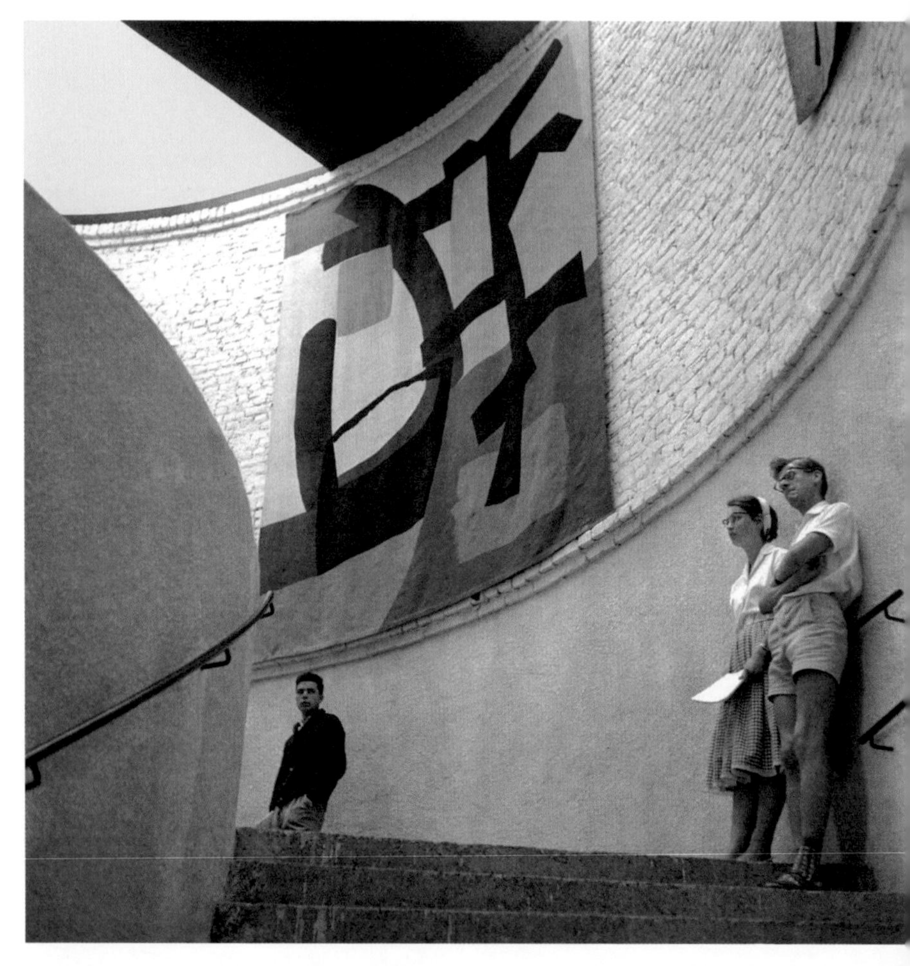